MODERN WORLD CULTURES

Africa South of the Sahara

◆

Australia and the Pacific

◆

East Asia

◆

Europe

◆

Latin America

◆

North Africa and the Middle East

◆

Northern America

◆

Russia and
the Former Soviet Republics

◆

South Asia

◆

Southeast Asia

◆

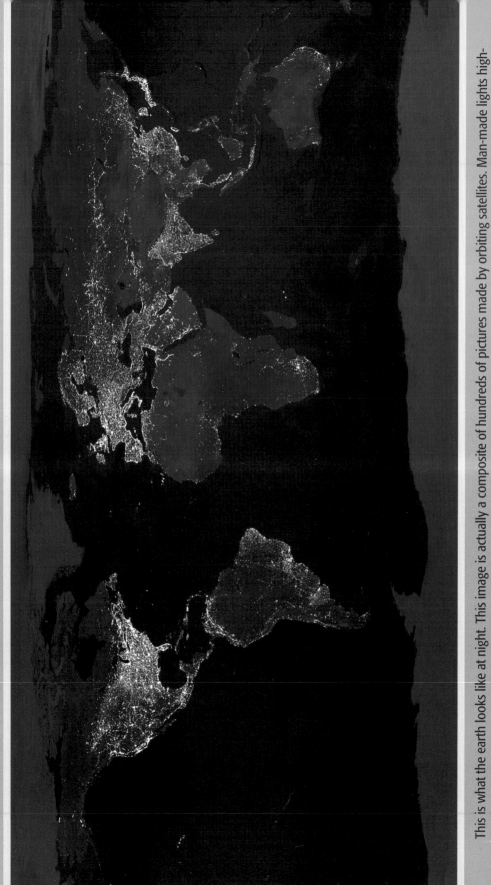

This is what the earth looks like at night. This image is actually a composite of hundreds of pictures made by orbiting satellites. Man-made lights highlight the developed or populated areas of the earth's surface. The dark areas include the central parts of South America, Africa, Asia, and Australia.

(Credit: C. Mayhew and R. Simmon; NASA/GSFC, NOAA/NGDC, DMSP Digital Archive.)

Russia and the Former Soviet Republics

Thomas R. McCray
University of Missouri, Columbia

Series Consulting Editor
Charles F. Gritzner
South Dakota State University

CHELSEA HOUSE
PUBLISHERS
An imprint of Infobase Publishing

Cover: Ice fishing on the Volga River

Russia and the Former Soviet Republics

Chelsea House
An imprint of Infobase Publishing
132 West 31st Street
New York NY 10001

Library of Congress Cataloging-in-Publication Data

McCray, Thomas R.
  Russia and the former Soviet republics / Thomas R. McCray
    p. cm. — (Modern world cultures)
  Includes bibliographical references and index.
  ISBN 0-7910-8144-3 (hard cover)
  1. Former Soviet republics. 2. Post-communism—Former Soviet republics. I. Title. II. Series.

  DK293.M35 2005
  947′.0009′051′1—dc22   2005015057

Chelsea House books are available at special discounts when purchased in bulk quantities for businesses, associations, institutions, or sales promotions. Please call our Special Sales Department in New York at (212) 967-8800 or (800) 322-8755.

You can find Chelsea House on the World Wide Web at http://www.chelseahouse.com

Text and cover design by Takeshi Takahashi

Printed in the United States of America

Bang MCC 10 9 8 7 6 5 4 3 2 1

This book is printed on acid-free paper.

All links and web addresses were checked and verified to be correct at the time of publication. Because of the dynamic nature of the web, some addresses and links may have changed since publication and may no longer be valid.

TABLE OF CONTENTS

Charles F. Gritzner

Geography is the key that unlocks the door to the world's wonders. There are, of course, many ways of viewing the world and its diverse physical and human features. In this series—MODERN WORLD CULTURES—the emphasis is on people and their cultures. As you step through the geographic door into the ten world cultures covered in this series, you will come to better know, understand, and appreciate the world's mosaic of peoples and how they live. You will see how different peoples adapt to, use, and change their natural environments. And you will be amazed at the vast differences in thinking, doing, and living practiced around the world. The MODERN WORLD CULTURES series was developed in response to many requests from librarians and teachers throughout the United States and Canada.

As you begin your reading tour of the world's major cultures, it is important that you understand three terms that are used throughout the series: geography, culture, and region. These words and their meanings are often misunderstood. **Geography** is an age-old way of viewing the varied features of Earth's surface. In fact, it is the oldest of the existing sciences! People have *always* had a need to know about and understand their surroundings. In times past, a people's world was their immediate surroundings; today, our world is global in scope. Events occuring half a world away can and often do have an immediate impact on our lives. If we, either individually or as a nation of peoples, are to be successful in the global community, it is essential that we know and understand our neighbors, regardless of who they are or where they may live.

Geography and history are similar in many ways; both are methodologies—distinct ways of viewing things and events. Historians are concerned with time, or when events happened. Geographers, on the other hand, are concerned with space, or where things are located. In essence, geographers ask: "What is where, why there, and why care?" in regard to various physical and human features of Earth's surface.

Culture has many definitions. For this series and for most geographers and anthropologists, it refers to a people's *way of life*. This means the totality of everything we possess because we are human, such as our ideas, beliefs, and customs, including language, religious beliefs, and all knowledge. Tools and skills also are an important aspect of culture. Different cultures, after all, have different types of technology and levels of technological attainment that they can use in performing various tasks. Finally, culture includes social interactions—the ways different people interact with one another individually and as groups.

Finally, the idea of **region** is one geographers use to organize and analyze geographic information spatially. A region is an area that is set apart from others on the basis of one or more unifying elements. Language, religion, and major types of economic activity are traits that often are used by geographers to separate one region from another. Most geographers, for example, see a cultural division between Northern, or Anglo, America and Latin America. That "line" is usually drawn at the U.S.-Mexico boundary, although there is a broad area of transition and no actual cultural line exists.

The ten culture regions presented in this series have been selected on the basis of their individuality, or uniqueness. As you tour the world's culture realms, you will learn something of their natural environment, history, and way of living. You will also learn about their population and settlement, how they govern themselves, and how they make their living. Finally, you will take a peek into the future in the hope of identifying each region's challenges and prospects. Enjoy your trip!

Charles F. "Fritz" Gritzner
Department of Geography
South Dakota State University
May 2005

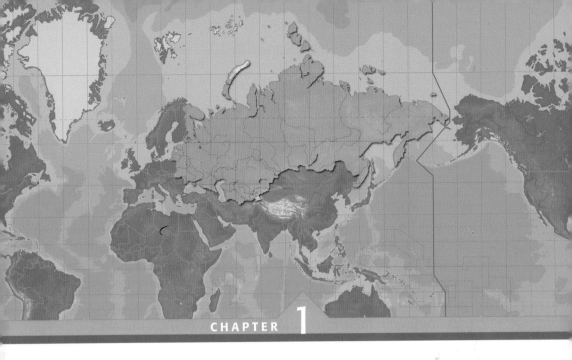

CHAPTER 1

Introducing Russia and the Former Soviet Republics

RUSSIA—A HEARTLAND IN TRANSITION

This book examines a country and culture at the core of a great political realm. It was a realm of Eastern Slavic tribes 1,000 years ago, of the Russian Empire for 500 years, and of the Union of Soviet Socialist Republics (the Soviet Union, or USSR) for most of the twentieth century. It involved the Vikings' conquest over a Slavic people and the emergence of the first Russians. It rose to world fame on the vision of single-minded tyrants, on the strength of artists, explorers, and engineers, and on the hard labor of oppressed workers and colonized foreigners. Toward the end of the twentieth century, it lost its grip on an immense empire of captive nations in a cascade of defections and retreats that left the world amazed.

On December 25, 1991, the general secretary of the Communist Party of the USSR resigned; the next day the Soviet Union broke up. Arguably the strongest military power on Earth simply disappeared. It was one of history's greatest political disintegrations. At the center of this great collapse, the Russian Federation remains intact. The "new" Russia has a population of 145 million people and a strong sense of cultural identity. It remains the world's largest country in area and constitutes perhaps its own surviving internal empire.

Sweeping around Russia's west and south are the other 14 former Soviet republics. Many of these now-independent countries are forging new international relations beyond the old empire. Most of them also remain closely tied to Russia. They are as diverse as any collection of states on Earth, but they all recently acquired their independence. The modern Baltic Republics—Estonia, Latvia, and Lithuania—recently were accepted as members of the European Union. To the southwest are the Republic of Belarus, which questions its separation from Russia, Moldova, which is still trying to assert its independence, and Ukraine, which is celebrating its freedom. In the Caucasus Mountains south of Russia, Georgia is a fragmented state, Armenia regains its legendary isolation, and Azerbaijan is fighting a war with Armenia over controversial borders drawn in Soviet times. Farther east, beyond the Caspian Sea, Kazakhstan and Uzbekistan deal with large non-Kazakh and non-Uzbek populations, respectively. Turkmenistan is run by a tight central leadership, and Tajikistan and Kyrgyzstan search for outside support.

Even before the collapse of the USSR, a looser confederation was proposed. At that time, most of the former Soviet republics formed the Commonwealth of Independent States (CIS). Only westward-facing Estonia, Latvia, and Lithuania have refused to take any part in the organization. The goals of CIS were stated in lofty terms: to endorse equality, to strengthen friendship and cooperation, to promote human rights, and to protect the peace. The real purpose of CIS, however, was to continue running

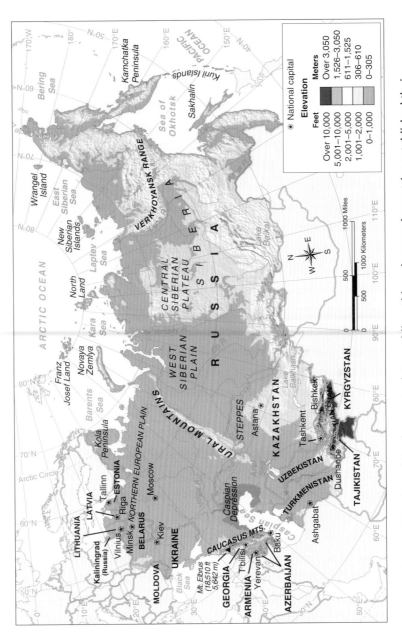

A general map of Russia and the former Soviet republics. Although several countries established their independence following the collapse of the Soviet Union, Russia maintains a vast expanse of land.

member economies in the absence of a single authority. Member states had practically never known independence. Many of their borders were, and still are, vague, and they had no developed defenses. Their economies were mostly directed from Moscow. All of them shared transportation and telecommunications networks that were designed to keep them codependent and tied to Russia, which never intended to integrate any single republic internally. Today, the CIS is weak. Member countries use it but do not put resources into it. Trade with countries that lie far away and were not part of the USSR is preferred.

Inside Russia, 80 percent of the people are Russian. Most non-Russians are Muslim, and this worries some Russians. For centuries, Muslims and Russians have been engaged in on-and-off conflicts. Whether Tatars, Mongols, Turks, or another group of Muslims, Islam does battle with Russian Orthodoxy. Today, tensions between Russians and Muslims continue to boil.

How do the non-Russians feel? In a word, they are nervous. During and after the Soviet breakup, the people of Russia did not know how tightly or how freely they would be governed in their new state. A crush of groups claimed their own natural resources, foreign policies, and even independence. Russia was starting to tear apart, but Russia is overwhelmingly Russian and Russians do not want their country torn apart. Early in the twenty-first century, a popular national government has gradually and deliberately pulled and tucked the whole country back into compliance with Moscow. That policy spoils the hopes of people in places such as Tatarstan, Tuva, Bashkortostan, Buryatia, Sakha, and Chechnya. These regions are unknown to most Americans, but for Russians they represent a challenge to the federation and their moods deserve close watching.

In the other former Soviet republics, 23 million Russians still live where they did when the Soviet Union disintegrated. What will become of them? They were trained to serve a system that no longer exists, and systems that exist now have no places

August 22 is remembered in Russia as the anniversary of the suppression of anti-democratic forces in 1991. The Day of the National Flag was instituted as a national holiday by President Boris Yeltsin.

for them. In several non-Russian republics, Russians make up sizeable percentages of the population. Their dissatisfaction, or an outright revolt, could destabilize their host country. Russia has pledged to help them, but how to do so remains uncertain. As is the case with minorities inside Russia, the status of Russians in the non-Russian former republics is uncertain.

Russia commands the heartland of Earth's greatest land-mass. This was true in 1900, when the British navy could not touch it. It was true in the Cold War, when the United States tried to contain it. It is true today as revolutions swirl around it. As far as we can predict, Russia will be at the center of great change. However, because of its difficult physical environment, because of a national preoccupation with survival, because of its ponderous governments, and because of its conflicting self

Vendors sell *matryoshka*, or nesting dolls, on the street in Moscow. Traditionally a child's toy, the first *matryoshka* doll reflected the image of a healthy peasant girl, with similar images on the dolls within.

images, Russia will be slow to change. The people of the United States were hoping for faster progress, for greater prosperity, and for closer cooperation out of Russia. Everyone hoped for a greater peace dividend from lowered military spending. As a result of leaders meeting, institutions taking root, and elections becoming more routine, a line between suspicion and partnership has been crossed, but it has not been a clear line. The popular Russian nesting dolls, called *matryoshka*, reveal one thing inside another inside another. Russians know this dissembling feeling.

The Russian region is a complicated place both inside and out. Beyond the arc of former republics are Eastern European countries that suffered under the Soviet Union and Asian countries that fiercely resisted it. Today's Russia borders 14 foreign countries, with another nine located on opposite shores of intervening waters. Among these neighboring countries are some of the world's richest, poorest, most populous, least stable, most dynamic, and least free. Clearly, Russia retains its central position. It is a window on the world and destined, to be a world player.

The greatness of a culture reflects the tenacity of its people, and Russians are gloriously tenacious. Extreme winters, an enormous country, and terrible wars forged a people that is practiced in survival. Russian culture is grand and powerful. Russian music, poetry, sculpture, and painting are often serious, withdrawn, and even brooding. They are also exciting, shocking, and huge. The West (primarily capitalist Western Europe and North America) may have a long lead in matters of business and industry, but cultured Westerners often turn to Russian authors and composers for a taste of deep emotion and soaring inspiration.

The chapters that follow examine the rise of the Russian people and seek an understanding of what makes them special. This book tours their vast country and considers their relationship with the land. The text reviews Russia's recent climb to independence and considers what this means for individual Russians and for their nation. It considers Russian relations with the world community and where those may lead. The Soviet Union is gone. Russians tell us that their country was not their own under the USSR. What can they make of it now?

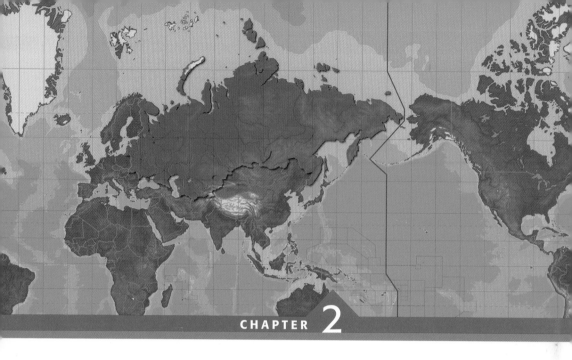

CHAPTER 2

Physical Geography

THE SETTING

To most readers, *Russia* is an abstract term, like *China, India,* and *Arabia.* This is a good place to start our study, because Russia, as much as any place on Earth, is practically an abstraction. It is so big that you could never walk all of it, and so remote that you could never drive all of it. There are still places in remote Russia where no person has ever been.

Russians are European, but most of Russia is in Asia. The Ural Mountains form the boundary between the two continents, but there is little physical support for this assignment. The Urals are a low range that is easily crossed, and a traveler does not experience any sudden shift in culture when crossing them. Since the reforms of Peter the

Great in the early eighteenth century, however, the Russians and other European leaders have sought to move Europe's eastern frontier farther eastward. Three hundred years ago, it was Poland. Now, it is the Urals. Russia has one foot in each world, east and west, and the Russians' identification with one or the other tends to follow the government's policies of reform or isolation.

Russia is a big country. When measured north to south, it spans an area comparable to that of Canada, China, or the United States. When measured west to east, however, Russia simply cannot be compared with any other country. It spreads out nearly halfway around the world and spans 11 time zones (the continental United States spans 4). In North America, the Rockies channel weather southward from the Arctic or northward from the tropics into the interior of the continent. In Russia, the biggest mountain barriers lie roughly along the southern borders, blocking invasions of warm tropical air. From the north, Russia offers a wide open door to Arctic air, so that the world's most enduring image of Russia is the cold.

LAND FEATURES
The West

This survey of Russia's major landforms begins in the west. Here, Russia occupies a large portion of the East European (or Russian) Plain. This gently rolling land feature stretches from the Baltic Sea in the north to the Black Sea in the south. From west to east, it gradually slopes downward from the Carpathian Mountains to the Volga River Basin. The Valdai Hills (west and slightly north of Moscow) are an important highlight of this plain. Several important Russian rivers begin on this gentle rise and flow outward in different directions. For this reason, early explorers traveled upstream on one river and then had to lift their boats out of that stream and portage them (move them over land) on rolling logs to another stream.

The 350-year-old Tutayevsky Cathedral sits next to the Volga River. This south-flowing river is one of Russia's most important waterways.

East of the Valdai Hills, the great Russian Plain is dissected by north-flowing rivers of limited utility and also by two very important south-flowing rivers. These two, the Don and Volga rivers, are very important in Russia's historic development and for its ongoing economy. The streams flow to Russia's warmest areas with the longest growing seasons.

The Volga River

The Volga is a pivotal landmark in the life of the Russian nation. Throughout the twentieth century, the Russians have tested themselves against the Volga, and the river has suffered. From 1937 to 1958, eight major hydroelectric dams were built on the Volga, and another three were built on the Kama River. Major canals and other dredging projects were also completed during this time. These enabled commercial and military ships to connect the Baltic and White seas in the north with the Caspian and Black seas in the south.

Unfortunately, all of the attention paid to the Volga has had an adverse effect. Fertilizer and pesticide runoff combine with factory and municipal wastes to pull oxygen out of the water and replace it with heavy metals. Car owners wash their cars, and farmers wash their tractors in the river, leaving oil and grease running downstream. Polluting plants in Volgograd and Astrakhan dust the river with carbon and sulfur.

Nearly half of the Volga's water is held in reservoirs behind the river's many dams. This has resulted in a drop in water temperature, making the water less beneficial for irrigating crops. The disadvantage is not offset by the 22 aging nuclear power plants that pour heated water back into the river. Because of the many dams, the river's velocity is slowed to 10 percent of its natural speed. Slower flow means that spawning gravels for migrating fish are often silted over. Critical spring freshwater flow is 40 percent below natural levels. Historic 1,250-mile (2,000-kilometer) fish migrations now stop at Volgograd Dam, just 125 miles (200 kilometers) upstream. Some confused fish manage to climb the fish ladders, only to discharge their eggs on the muddy riverbed, where they are often exposed by low water. The famous sturgeon catch (the source of Russian caviar) declined by 50 percent from 1938 to 1960. By the mid-1980s, an estimated 70 percent of fish in the Lower Volga were sick. The Ural River now has more natural fish nursery grounds than the much larger Lower Volga.

East of the Volga, the land rises gradually toward the Ural Mountains, an important zone of Russian industry and the jumping-off point to Siberia. This is the Volga Foreland, a primary oil-producing area since the 1950s. Huge factories and refineries were built here in the infamous model of Soviet excess. Several of them were the largest plants in the world.

The East

The vast—and, to most Russians, forbidding—territory of Siberia lies east of the Urals. Immediately east of the Urals lies the West Siberian Lowland. This is a marshy expanse of mosquitoes, oil, and natural gas, with a serious river problem that is typical for Siberia. The problem is that the the Ob River System flows from south to north, while the advancing spring melt also moves from south to north. Unfortunately, water moves faster than the change of seasons, resulting in spring meltwater crashing into frozen river water as it runs downstream (northward). At this point, the rivers rise over their banks. Because of this annual progression of ice jams, vast lowland areas are typically flooded every year. At the eastern margin of this broad basin, the Yenisey River rolls northward, and, like the Ob, it ultimately pours into the Kara Sea.

The Kara Sea

The Kara Sea is not a familiar feature to most Americans, but it should be. Here's why: The Arctic ice cap is formed mostly from frozen freshwater rather than from seawater. The Yenisey and Ob rivers, with a combined discharge nearly one and a half times that of the Mississippi, flow into the Kara Sea. This freshwater forms most of the Arctic sea ice.

The Kara Sea also warrants attention because, for more than 100 years, Russians have proposed diverting water from the Ob southward to the parched lands of Central Asia. This warmer region has been important for many years because it can grow warm-weather crops such as cotton. Further agricultural development has been hampered by the shortage of freshwater in the area. If the Ob's flow could be redirected from the Arctic to watering thirsty cotton, the argument goes, everyone would benefit. This, however, would cause a serious problem. A reduced polar ice pack would reflect less sunlight into space and absorb more heat at the surface. This, in turn, would contribute to global warming. It even seems doubtful that much of the water sent southward would survive seepage and evaporation to reach Central Asia. The plan has been rejected on several occasions, mostly for lack of financing, but it keeps coming up—most recently in 2002. This unlikely dream for interbasin water transfer is one example of the Russians' environmental carelessness that was all too common in the twentieth century.

Farther east, the Central Siberian Plateau is one of the world's pivotal landforms. Reading a physical map northward from the Indian Ocean, one sees the Indian subcontinent pushing into Asia and uplifting the Himalayas and Tibetan Plateau. Then, the Tarim Basin of Western China drops, and the Sayan and Yablonovyy Mountains of southern Russia rise on opposite sides of Lake Baikal. At the northern end of all of this folding and faulting is the hard rock shield of Central Siberia. This is an exposed remnant of the first continent, Pangaea, and its age is measured to 3.5 billion years.

Lake Baikal

Lake Baikal, located at the southern margin of the Central Siberian Plateau, merits special attention. It is the oldest and deepest lake on Earth, and it contains a staggering 20 percent of the world's liquid freshwater—300 cubic miles (1,250 cubic kilometers) more water than all of North America's Great Lakes combined. On Baikal, the ice freezes so deeply that freight trains were driven over it to supply the Russo-Japanese War of 1905. Lake Baikal, nicknamed the "Pearl of Siberia," is famous for its pristine, oxygen-rich water. It is so clear that a shiny object can easily be seen at depths of 100 feet. Summer days can hit 80°F (27°C), but the surface water of Baikal stays refreshingly cool. Because of its great age (thought to exceed 30 million years) and its isolation, Baikal is resplendent with life. Swimmers encounter schools of little fish that come to nibble salt from human skin. Baikal is home to 1,500 species of fish and plant life found nowhere else on Earth, including a rare freshwater seal called the "nerpa."

The Baikal, or "nerpa," seal is a freshwater seal that lives in Baikal, the world's deepest lake. The nerpa and other rare species that inhabit Lake Baikal have recently been threatened by increasing amounts of pollution in the lake.

In the mid-1950s, the Soviets' zeal for mastering the environment came to Baikal. Surely, the Russians believed, Baikal's size would counteract any effects by man. The nearly pure waters of Baikal came under increasing attack from cellulose-processing plants, whose product was used in making tires and clothing. Their acidic waste was dumped directly into Baikal. The lake also suffers from small, but dangerous, runoff of chemical and municipal waste streams and from 60 years of logging operations. Floating logs sometimes sink, and their acidic decay exceeds levels of natural occurrence. This pollution has been doubly dangerous for the rare species of Lake Baikal, because, although the lake has hundreds of streams feeding into it, there is only one running out of it. Pollutants that enter Baikal can be expected to stay and circulate for an average period of 400 years.

The effects of pollution became evident in the 1980s. Unnatural algae began to spread, tiny shrimp began to die, and abnormal fat samples were taken from nerpa seals. Fortunately for Lake Baikal, the Russian industrial economy practically collapsed in the 1990s. Demand for high-performance tires fell off and logging operations near the lake slowed. It is ironic that Russia's economic downturn reversed environmental declines at Lake Baikal and elsewhere.

The Far East

Beyond Central Siberia lies a wild country that Russians vaguely call the Far East. It is composed largely of a series of north-south mountain ranges and north-flowing rivers. Here, advancing from the east-southeast, the Pacific Plate is subducting (tucking under) the Asian landmass and raising these mountains. Here, too, west of the broad Lena River Basin, is that stubborn backstop of the Central Siberian Plateau.

Southern Plains

Arching around southern and southwestern Russia are broad plains. Much of the food for the former USSR was grown here. Today, however, most of this land lies in independent, non-Russian territories of the former Soviet Union. Much of this land lies in Ukraine and Kazakhstan. Enormous stocks of oil and natural gas were recently discovered under Kazakhstan's plains and its share of the Caspian Sea. Kazakhstan will capitalize on this wealth in accordance with its ability to export these fossil fuels across neighboring state territories. Ukraine once held great stocks of high-quality coal. However the shallowest coal seams are now mined out, and Ukraine is left with its greatest asset—good farmland. Together, these two republics further separate Russia from the rest of the world, and they are sorely missed by the old Russian empire builders.

CLIMATE REGIONS
Tundra

With the country's long, generally rectangular shape and relatively few physical barriers to the westerly winds, Russia's climatic and vegetative regions stack up in horizontal belts. The northernmost belt, which hugs the Arctic coastline, is Arctic tundra. This is a punishing environment of ripping winds and very short summers. There is almost no soil here, because there is practically no worm population to cultivate it. In addition, the ground at shallow depth is permanently frozen into what is called "permafrost." No large trees can sink their roots into the permafrost, and water does not percolate through it. Most of the region experiences only a month or two with average temperatures above freezing. Only scrubby mosses and lichens can survive in these cold conditions and short growing seasons. The brief summer thaw also creates a boggy surface, where huge mosquito colonies attract large seasonal bird migrations.

Taiga

South of the tundra is the broad belt of subarctic taiga. The most visible sign of transition from tundra to taiga is the appearance of taller trees, owing to longer growing seasons and deeper root penetration into the permafrost. In fact, Russia's taiga is home to a great boreal (northern) forest of needleleaf cone-bearing trees, including spruce, fir, larch, and pine. This taiga belt stretches across Russia from the Baltic Sea to the Pacific Ocean, making it the world's largest forest.

Despite its appearance, the taiga zone is not a place where trees grow easily. Vegetation barely grows when temperatures average below 42°F (5.5°C), and the taiga experiences at least six months below 32°F (0°C). Another problem is that the trees

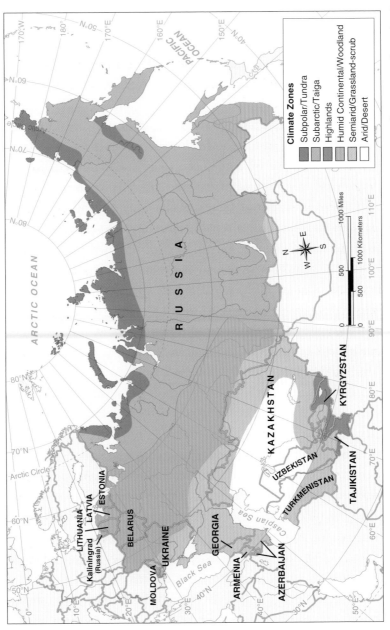

This is a climate map of Russia and the former Soviet republics. Most of the countries lie to the west and south of Russia and climates range from arid desert to humid woodland. Although Russia contains similar climates where it borders these other countries, the climate of its interior is primarily subpolar and subarctic.

must survive on thin, acidic soils. Taiga soils reflect, in part, the perpetual mat of rotting needles dropped by the forest, whose acids leach other soil nutrients down and away from the root zone. Russian taiga soils frequently overlie permafrost, which forces the trees to spread their roots laterally and interlace with mosses and fungi that survive on the forest floor. These small plants channel moisture to the tree roots, and as they die and decay they feed the forest.

Russia has a treasure trove of natural resources, including the taiga. Since gaining independence, Russia has sold taiga timber and pulpwood abroad at an accelerated rate. As a result, entire communities of plants and animals are beginning to suffer. By 2002, it was believed that only a small portion of Russia's European taiga remained intact, and very little of that is protected by law. It is easy to be deceived by the sheer size of this land. Surely, it seems, such a place can absorb the puny impacts of man. Because of this reasoning, environmental protection has been slow to gain favor in Russia. The taiga situation, however, refutes traditional thinking. As big as it is, the taiga is a slow-growing resource because of the temperature and soil problems already discussed.

Larch is one of the most common trees found in the taiga ecosystem and permafrost environment. It is unique. Nearly all needleleaf trees in North America are evergreen, so Americans are surprised by a larch forest. The larch is deciduous, so it grows needles in the spring and summer before changing colors and dropping its foliage in the fall. This cycle means that a forest where larch grows is an extremely acidic place, generally only suitable for that particular tree. With its shallow root penetration, a larch forest tends to feature leaning and tilting trees blown over by storms, and the Russians sometimes call it a "drunken forest." The Russians would like to sell more larch, but buyers are reluctant, because the slow-growing and tipsy larch is resinous, knotty, and difficult to mill into useful lumber. Its tight growth rings make it a very dense wood, so it sinks and is difficult to move on water. Railroads to the taiga interior would make the larch more marketable, but permafrost creates one of the world's most difficult building surfaces. During summer months, the thawed upper surface becomes spongy, making it very costly to build on.

The taiga is also a region of extreme seasonality, where temperatures can swing more than 100°F (38°C) between winter and summer. In Verkhoyansk, for instance, where the temperature has fallen to −91°F (−68°C), July days typically approach 80°F (27°C). As is the tundra, taiga wetlands are favorite breeding grounds for migratory birds. Those wetlands abound. Just in the Western Siberian Lowland, swampland covers an area of nearly half a million square miles (1.3 million square kilometers), and its size increases annually.

West of the Urals, the climate regions are generally less extreme. Tundra and taiga still cover the northern half of European Russia, but in Europe, the taiga has a longer growing season, more consistent rainfall, and a more balanced mix of trees. Needleleaf fir, spruce, and pine in the north give way to a transitional zone of broadleaf deciduous oak, ash, willow, alder, and birch. With so much leaf litter, mature brownish-colored soils have developed on this middle tier of European Russia. The climate of the Volga basin and the Russian Plain is reminiscent of Montana, Wyoming, or the Dakotas, and farmers grow barley, oats, rye, and pasture grasses.

Steppe

To the south of European Russia's mixed forest runs a band of steppe grasslands. This area has the most fertile soil in all of Russia. The rich *chernozem* (black earth) is formed by countless seasons of grass having built up the soil's high organic content. Chernozem soils occur mainly within an area bounded by the cities of Kursk and Ufa in the north and Stavropol in the south. It is not a continuous zone, and Russia lost access to a lot of its chernozem when Ukraine and

Kazakhstan became independent. Russia's remaining black earth is its most-plowed agricultural zone. It yields good returns of vegetables and fruits, winter and spring wheat, sunflowers, sugar beets, barley, and even corn, where moisture is adequate.

Settlement

In terms of settlement, physical features often limit or encourage the expansion of a nation. Through their formative years, Russians operated only on the eastern plains and valleys of Europe, much like the Americans clung to the Atlantic seaboard until the mid-1800s. The eighteenth and nineteenth centuries saw a wave of Russian explorers reach all the way to the opposite shore. While the Americans moved west, the Russians moved east. In the United States, progress was measured by crossing great north-south barriers: The Appalachians; the Great Plains; the Rockies; and the Sierra Nevadas. For the Russians, however, national progress was consistently measured by their control of rivers. Rivers were the arteries of the nation, moving people, goods, and ideas, as well as water. For 400 years, practically until the twentieth century, Moscow's dominance over all other Russian cities was achieved through its central access to rivers.

LIMITATIONS ON AGRICULTURE

One of the world's oldest and most essential human industries is agriculture. Every sovereign country must account for it. In Russia, most agriculture—in fact, most human activity of all types—takes place within a giant imaginary triangle. This region is roughly contained within boundaries drawn between St. Petersburg in the northwest, the Russian Black Sea coast in the south, and Novosibirsk in the east. Agriculture is certainly not continuous throughout this wedge; in places, there are mountains and swamplands to contend with.

Farmers take a meal break in the fields of the Novosibirsk region. Russia depends heavily on the agriculture of this region, which has a short growing season because of its severe weather.

Types of agriculture vary greatly throughout the region. The "breadbasket of the Soviet Union" is what people once called "Ukraine." Kazakhstan supports sprawling wheat fields reminiscent of farms on America's Great Plains. Now, Russia's most valuable farmland (some of which is irrigated) is found in an area the size of Kansas laid out between these two near-abroad countries in this region's southernmost area. Other near-abroad states, Belarus in Europe and Uzbekistan in Central Asia, also used to export quantities of meat, grain, and cotton to the rest of the Soviet Union. Today, however, most of their sales are to other countries and Russia is increasingly reliant on its southern lands and the Volga basin.

Farther north, hearty grains (barley, oats, and rye), potatoes, beets, timber, and flax (for linen) are harvested, and dairying is important. East of the Urals, wheat and animal feed grains are planted, and cattle are grazed for their meat. Outside of the wedge, only a few small areas are significantly farmed. An outside observer is struck by the huge parts of Russia that still are not exploited for food or fiber.

Despite its great size and able population, Russian agriculture is challenged by several environmental restrictions. First and most obvious is that so much of Russia is situated in far-northern latitudes. Most of the country experiences long, cold winters and short summers that offer a limited growing season.

Second, because the Russian landmass is so big, it practically generates its own weather. It is important to remember that all of Russia's southern and warmer climates are far from the moderating effects of an ocean. Therefore, cold, heavy winter air forces high pressure onto the surface and prevents the inflow of warmer air into the region. Regenerating cold cells, thus, turn deep winters into ultra-deep winters, shortening the growing season and limiting the variety of crops that can be grown. In summer, the lands of southern Russia, and especially of the former-Soviet Central Asian republics, become very hot. These hot-air regions experience lifting air, so that hot, dry air masses rush into the cores of low-pressure centers. These hot, dry winds (called *sukhovey*) can wither crops in a matter of hours. Seasonal temperature and pressure extremes occur in Russia and Central Asia because of "continentality." Simply stated, land heats and cools faster and to a greater extreme than water does. This is why Seattle, which is farther north than Chicago, stays warmer in winter and cooler in summer than the Midwestern city. Most of Russia lies far from the world's oceans. Much of it is also walled off from warmer waters to the south by high mountain barriers.

A third cause of Russia's limited agricultural potential is a serious lack of water. This might seem odd, because only Brazil has more freshwater than Russia. Russia's water problem lies not in amount but rather in distribution. Only one major river, the Volga, delivers water from the cold north to the warmer south, where irrigation can bring substantial harvests of vegetables and fruits. All of Russia's other great river systems are located in Siberia, where the extreme climate prevents high-value farming. More than 80 percent of Russia's freshwater flows to the Arctic Ocean and, to a lesser degree, into the Pacific. Sadly, Russian lands that are hot enough for agriculture are not wet enough, and lands that are wet enough are not hot enough. Despite being nearly twice the size of the United States, Russia has only about two-thirds as much agricultural land. Only 7 percent of Russia can be farmed, compared to about 20 percent of the United States.

CHAPTER 3

Historical Geography

The world has seen great empires come and go—the Egyptian, Roman, Mongol, and British, to name a few. These empires and many others grew to enormous extents before falling back into the more familiar sizes and shapes that are familiar to us today. Russia, however, has survived for centuries as an imperial colossus.

TRAPPED BETWEEN TWO WORLDS

The story of Russia can be told reliably from the mid-800s—more than 1,100 years ago. As with great cultures around the world, however, idealized Russian history reaches back far beyond what is known to a legendary past that bolsters its national identity. Prehistoric humans are known to have migrated over the region of today's

European Russia before the Mediterranean Bronze- and Iron-Age civilizations left them competitively disadvantaged. About 2,800 years ago, Asian tribes entered the area from China, Mongolia, and Southern Siberia, trapping, hunting and farming parts of these new lands. Russia's story, therefore, interacts with that of these Asian tribes, and it unfolds at the center of a clash between the Eastern and Western worlds cultures. This bridge between cultural traditions connects to an ongoing struggle in the hearts of Russians even today.

Russians trace their national story back to the time of Noah and his ark. It is said that, of Noah's four sons, Japeth was given the lands of the north, including that of the Eastern Slavs—precursors of the Russians. Eastern Slavs spread out from west of the Dnieper River and divided into several tribes that scattered over the lands north and west of today's Moscow. As fraternal tribes often do, and as the Russian Chronicles recount, they competed bitterly for resources and power, weakening themselves in the process. In about 200 A.D., they fell to the Baltic and Germanic Goths. Over the next few centuries, they were conquered by the powerful Mongol Huns, led by Attila, then by the Mongol Avars and the Khazars. Between attacks, the Slavs pushed their own domain outward. In such a busy area, it became apparent that the Russians needed cover. Eventually, they sought the guidance and council of a great and powerful nation to the north—the Varangians, known also as the Vikings. This was a fateful invitation.

THE VARANGIAN LINK AND DAWN OF THE RUS

In about 860, the Varangians sent a man named Rurik to lead the Russians. From Novgorod, on the shores of Lake Ilmen, Rurik did not empower the Slavs, he conquered them—after all, the Varangians were great conquerors of their day. The Varangians were also successful mariners and traders. For them, these Eastern Slavs merely occupied a region between

This monument in St. Petersburg depicts Rurik, a Varangian prince, and his son, Igor. Rurik is known as the founder of the Rurik dynasty of Kievan Rus. Most Russian princes traced their lineage to him.

themselves and another great trading and seafaring people, the Greeks, at Byzantium. Rivers between these great powers would connect the Scandinavian-controlled Baltic Sea to the Greek-held Black Sea coast. The route was difficult. Slavs were forced to tow long boats along the shore and carry them around rocky shallow passages. They also had to push and pull boats along rolling log roads called "portages" between navigable headwaters. All the while, they had to fight off the various Mongol tribes that harassed these merchant fleets. It was a grueling life punctuated by terrible surprise attacks.

Slavs outnumbered Scandinavians and gradually blended with them, forming a new people called the "Rus." The Rus' directional thrust was to trade and conquer southward, mainly along the Dnieper River. After Rurik's rule ended, Oleg, the new leader, moved the capital to Kiev in about 880, and the state of Kievan Rus was born. Soon, there was a busy trading economy, moving furs, timber, honey, and wax southward and grain, fruits, wine, and salt north. With such complementary environments and resources in the north and south of Kievan Rus, its prosperity hinged on maintaining open trade between them. From this time on, the Russians were a recognized people. Kiev was their "Mother of Cities," and Oleg is regarded as their founder.

The fifth leader of Kievan Rus, Vladimir I, "the Great," studied other influential nations of his time and decided that his people needed a religion. This, he reasoned, would lift them from the level of "heathens" into the light of civilization. Vladimir's search for divinity may have been a politically calculated one. He shopped around and entertained representatives of Judaism, Islam, Western Christianity (Catholicism), and Eastern Christianity (Orthodoxy). Some practices were too austere for Vladimir, because he was a man of adventurous tastes. Others were too contemplative for the illiterate Rus. In Eastern Orthodoxy, Vladimir found a clear structure and wondrous ceremony to discipline and inspire his people. Accepting Orthodoxy also brought Kievan Rus closer to Byzantium, then the capital of Orthodox Religion and already a great city. In 988, Vladimir led his people into the Dnieper River and had them baptized. From that time forward, the Russians have been Orthodox Christians.

The next great leader, Yaroslav the Wise, presided over what was surely a golden age of Kievan Rus. He enacted the Russians' first legal code, built churches, promoted education, and improved foreign relations. Unfortunately for the Rus, however, Yaroslav's death in 1054 left the kingdom to his four contentious sons. Through their personal rivalries, Kievan Rus weakened and the Russians became vulnerable. Their feuding allowed western lands to break away, and it also allowed Tatar-Mongol horsemen to invade from the east and conquer most of their lands by 1300. These early Mongol Turks from north of

China (themselves mixed with other Asian tribes) proceeded to conquer lands deep into Europe.

Thus began a dark period that Russians call the "Mongol yoke," 240 years of control by Asian Khans. The most famous khan was the Mongol Chingis, also known as Genghis Khan, who assembled the largest land empire in history. The disorganized Russians did not have a chance against the powerful Mongols, so they escaped in the only direction the Asian horsemen would rather not go—northward into densely forested lands. For an army on horseback, open grassland is preferable to forested and swampy land. The Russians settled at a place deep in the woods and bogs of the Russian Plain: Moscow. There they paid tribute (taxes) to the khan and were generally left to themselves.

MOTHER VOLGA

There were other important Russian cities in the north, any of which might have become the new center of power. Moscow's princes defeated them all. They did this with such cruelty that a totalitarian standard attached itself to tsarist rule and even to the Soviet governments that came later. There were more humane and constructive ways to order a society, but Russia's survival essentially depended on strong central rule.

In the 1400s, the Turkic-Mongol Empire started to weaken under its own mass. In 1480, the Russians drove them off their southern doorstep by capturing the Oka River, barely 70 miles from Moscow. At this point, tribute payments ended and the Mongols went into retreat. In 1552 and 1556, commanded by their young Tsar Ivan IV, "the Terrible," Russians won two of their greatest victories—first against the Muslim Turks at Kazan, 450 miles east of Moscow, and then at Astrakhan, 800 miles to the south. In this process, the Turks were pushed south and east toward the Black Sea and into Central Asia. More importantly, Russia gained control of the Volga River.

It is impossible to overstate Russia's attachment to the Volga River. Taking "Mother Volga" from the Mongols was so important to the Russians that they marked the event on their most cherished symbol. Today, the unique bottom "T" on a Russian Orthodox cross represents the Volga victories of Orthodoxy (symbolized by the crucifix) over Islam (symbolized by the crescent moon). Never mind that the Golden Horde was made up of recent converts to Islam and that many were only marginally Muslim. Taking the Volga from the Mongols is the stuff of Russian legend. Here's why:

- By driving the Mongols back from the Volga, Russians blocked Mongol access to lands west of the Volga. The Asiatic threat to Europe retreated at this time.
- From Kazan, the Russians began to expand eastward, led by Cossack horsemen from the plains of Ukraine and southern Russia. These forces conquered lands all across Siberia—more than 4,000 miles—in less than 100 years. Their rapid expansion was managed largely through the use of Siberia's huge north-flowing rivers and lengthy portages between them. Later Russian empires crossed Siberia with a railroad and dammed its great rivers. Most Russians, however, would never see Siberia. For them, Volga remains the heartland.
- From Moscow, Russians reached outward to the Baltic, White, Caspian, and Black seas—all by way of the Volga. The Volga affirmed Moscow's place at the center of the Russian state.
- The Volga is itself a vast basin of arable farmland. By developing that basin, the Russians balanced their economy—moving grain and vegetables from the south and timber and hides from the north.
- *Vol* means "will" in Russian, and disciplining Volga came to represent Russia's mastery over self. Industrialization may have come slowly to tsarist Russia from Western Europe, but factory development along the Volga led the way—from 250 plants in 1725 to 2,000 in 1800. As a water highway, the Volga was, and still is, unsurpassed in Russia.

- The Volga gave the Russians a fallback position against Napoleon's invasion in 1812 and against the Germans in 1941. "Trading space for time" became Russia's core defensive strategy, as massive invasions from the east were replaced by massive invasions from the west. Time after time, Russia's immensity lured attackers in too far and winter shut the door behind them. Each time, the Volga protected and buffered the Russians.

ABSOLUTE RULE
Ivan the Terrible

Tsar Ivan IV wasn't called "the Terrible" (also "the Dread") for his conquering of the Volga, but rather for his unflinching grasp of state control. He was monstrous toward any institution that competed for power with his Moscow principality. He forced the Orthodox Church to finance and serve his will. He murdered and tortured members of the noble class of landowners, called *boyars,* and killed thousands in his attack on Novgorod. In 1565, he founded the *oprichniki* (secret police), and with it established a long tradition of Russian governments terrorizing their own people. He murdered his own son and more than one of his wives. His best years were past before his thirtieth birthday, and historians argue over his sanity in his later years. His power, however, and the power of tsars after him, was absolute.

With Russia spending centuries under Tatar-Mongol domination, the insult in Emperor Napoleon Bonaparte's observation "Scratch a Russian, find a Tatar" is clear. Bonaparte was French, or rather Corsican. (Corsica is an island in the Mediterranean that is governed as a region of France.) In any case, he was European and Latin, and Europe would survive Napoleon to reach an apex of invention, diplomacy, and civility. Russia, on the other hand, retained a social coarseness that set it apart from the Europe of evolving science, commerce, and democracy. Ivan IV slapped down the boyars (merchant class), but a lord-peasant social order stayed on. Today, ethnic associations are still stronger in Russia than in the United States and Western Europe, where vengeance and nepotism have been largely replaced by the rule of law. Russia's historic absence of freedom is often linked to its long interactions with tribal and despotic regimes.

Peter the Great

Among the great and dreaded tsars to follow was Peter I, "the Great," who traveled in Western Europe as a young man in the 1680s and returned home with ideas for a "modernized" Russia. He ordered the upper-class noblemen into state service and ordered that their children be educated. He built a strong navy and instituted a merit-based system of military promotions. He imposed Western fashions and manners on the members of his court—shaving beards, speaking French, and using forks and knives. He adopted the Julian calendar of the West and founded the Academy of Sciences. Peter wished for his empire to compete with the West more than to ally with the West. He was an apt student and a clever ruler. Peter simultaneously confronted Muslim revolutionaries in the Volga basin and Ukraine, defeated an uprising by disaffected military officers, and captured the eastern Baltic Sea from the powerful Swedes. Russia was suddenly respected on the European stage.

In 1703, Peter founded a new Russian capital, St. Petersburg. It was a classic Western capital, built of stone in the forested Russian north, where little stone exists. The city was situated on a tidal marshland, but it was also Russia's closest point to great Western cities of its time, especially London, Paris, and Amsterdam. Reminiscent of Vladimir the Great's embrace of Greek Orthodoxy, Peter turned Russia toward the West. No Russian theme is more telling than its almost cyclical preoccupation with Western culture. Revealing of Peter's tilt to Christianity is that St. Petersburg was not named for himself but for the Biblical apostle Peter. Thirty thousand peasants died building it.

A boat passes in front of the St. Isaak Cathedral in St. Petersburg during the "white nights." The period of the white nights occurs in June and attracts thousands of tourists to St. Petersburg. Because the city is so far north, the sun does not drop far enough below the horizon for the sky to get dark.

Catherine the Great

The next of Russia's greatest tsars, and another in a 300-year line of the Romanov family, was Catherine II, "the Great." Her rule ran from 1762 to 1796, and her greatest accomplishments resulted in her empire's expansion south and west. She was less successful at managing corruption in her own aristocratic circles and in gauging the opposition to serfdom (slavery). Catherine opposed democratic revolutions in the United States and France.

In terms of territory, Catherine's gains were dramatic. Russia took the northern Black Sea coast from the Turks, and it joined with Austria and Prussia (the precursor nation to Germany) in the total disintegration of Poland. Russia took Poland's eastern half that today is divided among independent Belarus and Ukraine.

Catherine toured the newly captured Crimean Peninsula in 1787. Her host for the tour was her appointed governor-general of southern Ukraine (and a personal favorite), Prince Grigory Aleksandrovich Potëmkin. The prince was said to make extravagant preparations for Catherine's visit, including pushing regional development schemes at an accelerated pace. Much of his village construction was apparently more started than finished at that time, and many thousands of peasants were just arriving for work in the fields. A busy and perhaps misleading impression nonetheless was made on Catherine. Many contend that Potëmkin deceived his empress with a false show of progress, and now any such hoax can be called a "Potëmkin village."

The Last Tsars

In 1861, two years before President Abraham Lincoln signed the Emancipation Proclamation in the United States, Tsar Alexander II freed the serfs. Yet in Russia, as in the United States, emancipation hardly improved the lot of the disenfranchised. Russia's serfs did not gain the means to sustain themselves. For the rest of the nineteenth century, their bad lives cost Imperial Russia the allegiance of more and more of its people. Even through the whole twentieth century, Russians continued to operate on some sort of lord-peasant social order.

In the late 1800s, Russia's great railroads were built and Russian industry spread away from the riverbanks to where important metal and mineral deposits came on line. The size of the empire started to come into focus. Russia's conquest of the Muslim khanates of Central Asia followed the United States's Civil War, Russia's sudden need for a new cotton supply, and concerns about British advances northward from India. It also contained a vengeful element, because the khanates of Central Asia were born of the Mongol empires and the Russians' Tatar yoke.

Although there was progress and Russia's immense territory continued to grow, most Russian people carried out dreary work in a brutal landscape and could only dream of a better life. There were, however, intellectuals and reactionaries with a

Revolutionary leader Vladimir Ilyich Lenin seized control of Russia in 1917. Under his leadership the communist government banned private ownership of property.

vision of human equality for Russia and the entire industrializing world. The last tsar, Nicholas II, turned back a revolution in 1905. He enacted major reforms, granting some land to peasants, recognizing a constitution, and ceding some authority to an elected *duma* (legislature). It wasn't enough. He seemed curiously unaware of the danger he faced.

IN THE SHADOW OF ABSOLUTE RULE
V.I. Lenin

In March 1917, a revolution drove the tsar from power and a more democratic Constituent Assembly was widely envisioned. On October 24, 1917, Vladimir Ilyich Ulyanov (who called himself "V.I. Lenin"), Lev Davidovich Bronstein (who went by the name "Trotsky"), and their band of Bolsheviks seized power. They dissolved competing political parties and established a one-party Communist dictatorship that lasted for 70 years.

Lenin and Trotsky ordered that private business and even private property be dissolved. Communism, they claimed, would place every person on an equal footing, regardless of personal talents. The state, managed by the Communist Party, would rule for the good of the people and determine what was to be done. The people would do it. The Communist Revolution was an idealistic reaction to the Industrial Revolution in the capitalist West. In the West, innovations were bringing a dramatic rise in living standards but also were spreading the division between the wealthy and impoverished classes. The Union of Soviet Socialist Republics, as it came to be called, would level the playing field for all citizens by divesting individuals of wealth and influence and empowering the state on behalf of all. Bolsheviks predicted that their revolution would sweep over Germany and even Great Britain before very long. In fact, their revolution did not spread.

Ultimately, the Communist system was neither wise nor fair enough to improve much on the Western model. Even in Russia, a multiyear civil war ensued. From Moscow, the Bolsheviks fought off fierce democrats and loyalists of the old regime. The tsar and his family were captured and executed on orders from Lenin. Lenin called for a quick redistribution of land to the peasants who worked it, but he and the early Communists were, in fact, contemptuous of the peasantry. By mid-1918, Lenin was taking away their votes and soon their land. The 1920s and 1930s were brutal years of collectivization, when government authorities crossed the countryside collecting the means of production—equipment, animals, and farmland—and assigning it all, together with the farms' workers and handlers, to newly established and state-owned collective farms.

Compliance with collectivization was spotty. Many farmers resisted turning over everything they had to a mysterious and unstable state system without receiving compensation.

Collectivization inspired many of the better farmers to destroy their harvests and kill their livestock rather than give them up to the Communists. These farmers were called *kulaks* for their selfish attitudes, and they were sent to wretched state prison camps (the *gulag*) hundreds or even thousands of miles away. Others were killed on the spot without even a hearing. The combined effects of collectivization, the devastation of World War I, and a serious drought in 1920 set the stage for a disastrous food shortage. It hit in 1921, and 10 million people starved to death.

Lenin, the Communist Party's first general secretary, recognized the need for a change of tactics. In 1921, he slowed collectivization and ordered the New Economic Policy, which allowed limited profits for business, small industry, and farming. With new incentives, workers returned to the fields, harvests were sent to market, and famine abated. Lenin had not renounced his Communist ideology, but he did temporarily step back from his faith in the masses to carry it out. He died in 1924.

Joseph Stalin

Trotsky may have been closer to Lenin ideologically, but it was the minister of nationalities, Joseph Stalin (a Georgian whose real name was Dzhugashvili) who elbowed his way into the general secretary's chair. The two men were terribly ambitious, and their rivalry deeply divided the Communist Party. Trotsky was more of a thinker whereas Stalin was a doer, and this rivalry brought about a bad end for Trotsky. He was stripped of his positions in 1926, expelled from the Communist Party in 1927, exiled to Siberia in 1928, and then exiled from the Soviet Union in 1929. He sought refuge in a number of foreign cities and continued to criticize Stalin's policies, until he was murdered in 1940, on a street in Mexico City. The crime was never solved.

Stalin, which means "steel" in Russian, became the face of the Soviet Union. For a quarter century, his energy and cruelty drove the USSR through enormous industrial campaigns, through the nightmare of World War II, and through a seem-

ingly endless cycle of mass arrests and secret executions for anyone conspiring against him or even making the slightest offensive reference to his leadership. His era was a reign of terror, and
yet the Soviet Union made great strides. Apparently, Western
capitalism would not be switching to Communism anytime
soon, so Stalin resolved to have a Communist Industrial Revolution in one country. Nothing like it had ever been seen before.

The USSR was put on a regimen of Five-Year Plans, which
involved the frenzied construction of huge dams, giant factories, long railroads, deep mines, and entire cities for new urban
workers. In their first decade, Soviet planners and builders
achieved results not seen elsewhere in 50 years. The inspiration
for all of this was not profit (no fortunes would be earned here),
but an endless stream of Communist Party propaganda.
Posters, articles, loudspeaker trucks, and even art and music
warned the people about aggressive capitalist enemies abroad
and dangerous counterrevolutionaries at home. In movies, pa-
rades, rallies, and rewritings of history, the working masses
were praised for their allegiance to the Communist Revolution
and for their love of the Soviet Motherland.

Stalin needed more food for his growing industrial population, so he discarded Lenin's New Economic Policy, with its cal-
ibrated incentives, and reinstituted forced collectivization. But
the taking of land, crops, animals, and equipment wasn't any
more successful under Stalin than it had been a decade earlier
under Lenin. Successful and productive farmers—those with
the most to lose—dodged the authorities, hid their profits, or
refused to work, making their contributions worthless.

Even Stalin relented a bit when he scolded his secret police
for being "dizzy with success." "Collectivization," he wrote,
"should be voluntary." Voluntary or not, however, collectivization under Stalin was pushed forward, and those who would
not comply were simply eliminated. Communist publications
denounced the killing of tens of millions of horses, cattle, sheep,
and pigs by greedy and subversive kulaks. The human toll can

only be imagined. After Stalin's death, it was revealed that collectivization had cost 15 million human lives.

World War II

It is difficult to comprehend the fear that gripped most Soviet citizens during this era of widespread terror and death. The Stalin era was also played out against the numbing backdrop of the two worst wars in history. No twentieth-century power was more ravaged by war than the USSR. In 1939, World War II had begun, but Stalin and Germany's Adolf Hitler signed a nonaggression pact. They then proceeded to divide up all of the countries in between them. Perhaps Stalin's pact with Hitler was unavoidable, because the USSR still was not strong enough to resist a militarizing Germany. Recognizing this weakness, Hitler violated the nonaggression pact and attacked the Soviet Union in June 1941. It was his greatest mistake. Like Napoleon had 140 years earlier, Hitler discovered that, for all his skills at directing a continental army, he could not grasp the vastness and severity of conditions in Russia.

The German army bogged down in the severe Russian winter and suffered its greatest setbacks on Russian soil. Nonetheless, the Soviet Union almost fell to the Germans in the war, and 20 million Soviets died, including 7 million civilians. To put this in perspective, the USSR lost 50 times more people than the United States lost. In Russia, it is called the Great Patriotic War, and veterans of that war still wear their medals everyday, and everywhere they go. There are memorials in every town and village (including the world's largest in Volgograd), and newly married couples still pay respect at war memorials on their wedding days.

After the war, Stalin suspected that some citizens had cooperated with the German invaders. As a result, he deported 1.4 million people, including ten entire ethnic groups, from southern Russia to gulag camps in Siberia and Kazakhstan. One-third to one-half of them died in transport, and the rest led grueling lives in the camps.

Soviet prison camps served several purposes. Of course, they rehabilitated or punished opponents of the regime. They also motivated the remaining "free" population to work harder and complain less, and they moved labor to distant worksites where no workers existed. Both Lenin and Stalin built up the gulags, and their system was a model for Hitler's infamous concentration camps. As with agriculture, higher wages or prices might have motivated workers to relocate, but Stalin would not corrupt his revolution with capitalistic tricks.

Throughout Stalin's 25 years in power, gulag populations grew, feeding on political dissidents and even loyal party members who differed with Stalin. There were religious people, "undesirable" minorities, and even people who had simply traveled abroad, as well as common criminals. Even Soviet soldiers taken prisoner by the German army were sent to gulags on their release at war's end. "Why," the suspicion went, "hadn't they died fighting?" As the demand for labor grew and Stalin's secret police kept rounding people up, prison populations passed 10 million in 1948 and continued to rise until Stalin's death in 1953. No one knows how many prisoners died in custody, but most estimates range from 7 million to 10 million.

CHAPTER 4

Population Geography

A HARD LEGACY

If one combines the deaths from forced collectivization and starvation with those from war, ethnic cleansing, and political punishment, the scale of early Soviet trauma begins to emerge. For the Slavic populations of the Soviet Union, a demographic disaster was in the making. Between 1940 and 1956, the U.S. population grew from 132 million to 169 million, a 22-percent increase. For the same period, the Soviet population grew from 192 million to 200 million, a gain of just 4 percent. War took a heavy toll on the number of men, resulting in fewer marriages and a sharp drop in births. This was particularly true among Slavic peoples. A generation later, birthrates were again low, reflecting an absence of potential parents who simply had not been born 20 years earlier. It is hard to predict, but if 40 million Soviet citizens had not died during the Stalin years and instead had produced 60 million babies in the 1950s and 1960s, and if they, in turn, produced 90 million babies in the 1970s and 1980s, then Russia would be a very different place today!

By the mid-1970s, it became clear that shifting birthrates threatened to overwhelm the Soviet Union with a majority of ethnic non-Russians. Russian and Ukrainian birthrates were very low, but Soviet Asian families—led by the Muslim Uzbeks, Tajiks, Azeris, and Turkmen—averaged five or six children each. In August 1991, when Ukraine seceded from the Soviet Union, 125 million Russians inside the Russian Republic faced the probability that their Slavic-dominated empire would slip away. Cultural preservation was of growing concern. The Baltic States were already gone, and Russia remained connected with the fast-growing populations to the south, not to mention Russia's internal Muslim regions. This threat to Russia's ethnic identity played a part in Russia's quitting the Soviet Union, resulting in the ultimate disintegration of the USSR.

Today, Russians and the other Slavic peoples of the former USSR are suffering population declines. A 2001 poll showed that 51 percent of Russians thought it best to have no more than one child. From suicide and poor health habits, the male life span has dropped from 72 years in the late 1980s to 60 years today. This is especially alarming for Russia, which already considers itself an underpopulated country. Russia is now approaching a condition where the youth population (17 and younger) is outnumbered by the retired population (65 and older), with pension and health-care costs falling on the shoulders of workers entering the work force. If current trends continue, Russia's population will shrink from 143 million (2005 estimate) to less than 120 million by 2050.

RUSSIA FOR RUSSIANS?

Russians like to remind themselves that they, just as much as any other group, were victims of the USSR. They claim that their

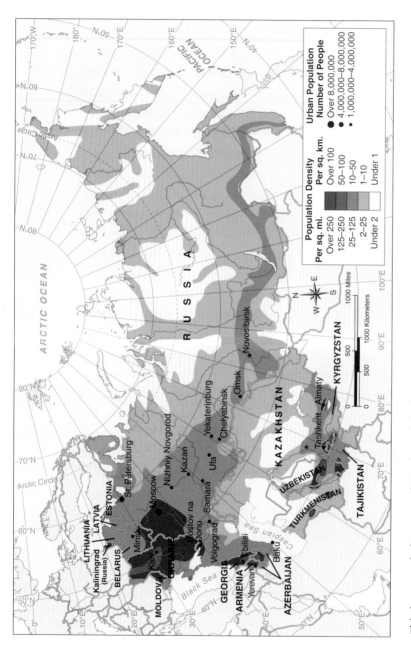

This is a population map of Russia and the former Soviet republics. The largest concentrations of people live in the southern and western parts of the region, where the climate is more hospitable.

own national identity was buried under the creation of the new "Soviet man." It was the Russians, however, who blended their identity into a national Soviet whole. Soviet leaders were most often Russian. Privileged positions were widely held by Russians, even in the non-Russian republics, and the USSR pushed Russification (primarily language and cultural training) on non-Russian minorities. It was the minorities who suffered the loss of control and esteem that came with the end of the USSR, so it is hard for Russians to deny that their spot was first among equals in the Soviet Union.

The Russians hardly lived like greedy colonists, however. From the time of Lenin on, they were encouraged to bury their nationalism and even their ethnicity beneath Soviet pride. This was not a successful policy for two reasons. First, everyone's personal identification document listed the individual's ethnicity. All Soviet citizens were required to carry and show these internal passports, so people were labeled and constantly reminded of their ethnic differences. Second, the "republics" of the USSR were all named for, and assigned to, their predominant ethnic group. Even within Russia (and within several of the other republics also), "autonomous regions" were set aside for outstanding ethnic groups, so that ethnicity was a political reality as well as a personal label.

In fact, the Soviet Union was a segregated place. Government policies separated people at least as much as they united them. The USSR was an empire. It held entire national groups together without their consent and ruled them all from Moscow, a distant place to most people. Now that the old union has broken apart along ethnic and political boundaries, those autonomous regions of Russia highlight the ethnic, religious, and cultural differences that exist among citizens of the Russian Federation. More than 100 different languages and dialects are spoken in Russia today; not all are spoken by willing subjects of the federation.

After the breakup of the USSR, Russia emerged with an 81 percent ethnic Russian population. This majority might be expected, inasmuch as the country is called the "Russian

Federation." Within the federation, autonomous regions have been elevated to republic status, and, again, ethnicity is the principle criterion for political separation. Today, in what is almost a replay of the Soviet predicament, many non-Russian peoples are struggling for greater freedoms inside Russia, and the Russian Federation is itself an empire.

In Siberia, there are the Yakut herdsmen, the Mongol Buryats, and the mountainous Tuvan people. Their religions and cultural traditions clash with those of the Russians, and they seek greater freedom and control over their natural resources. West of the Urals, many groups blend in comfortably with the Russians. Some others stand out for the ways they look, live, and believe. Along the Volga River, for example, the Muslim Tatar and Bashkir peoples have proclaimed their identities and their dissenting rights within the Russian Federation, and they struggle to assume sovereignty (the recognized control) over their homelands. They also live astride important oil and gas lines from Siberia, host important heavy industrial sites, and agitate for more control over the oil and gas being pumped from their republics. Conflict also stems from the fact that 11 million Russian citizens are Muslim.

Chechnya

The most volatile and rebellious region of Russia is the stretch of land north of the Caucasus Mountains. The most dangerous part of this area is Chechnya. The Muslim Chechens have never been willing partners with the Russians. In the nineteenth century, they fought for 60 years to resist Russian conquest. After the Russian empire fell in 1917, the Chechens fought bitterly to resist Soviet authority. When the Soviet Union collapsed, Chechens again proclaimed their independence. They have paid a terrible price for this resistance—nowhere more apparently than in their capital, Grozny. In the 1990s, Russian forces practically leveled this city and made it so unlivable that the only people remaining were those who could not leave.

Russia contains a wide variety of peoples and cultures. Visitors can find evidence of many of them along the streets of Moscow, where this man and his trained bear perform.

Russia's denial of Chechen self-determination certainly relates to Russia's own historic suffering under the Tatar-Mongol Muslims. It also has more recent justification. Throughout the Soviet period, the Chechens' resentment of the government inspired a culture of black marketeering and gangsterism. This reality has dehumanized Chechens in the eyes of many Russians. Since the mid-1990s, a series of savage terrorist attacks against Russians has implicated Chechens and practically destroyed the relations between these two peoples. Chechnya, moreover could not go free without igniting independence movements elsewhere in Russia, with dire consequences for Russia itself.

Despite its ethnic divisions, Russians are intent on holding their federation together—but many Russians also felt this way about the Soviet Union. In the end, they let it go, and their decision largely reflected the ethnic fault lines that ran through the USSR.

The Remains of the Union

When the Soviet Union broke up, 25 million Russians were left behind in non-Russian republics, and a comparable number of non-Russians were left living inside Russia. Now, however, on both sides of Russia's borders, nationalism is officially approved, and minorities clearly suffer from discrimination. Under the old Soviet system it was at least not supposed to happen. In Kazakhstan, Latvia, Estonia, and Ukraine, Russians make up 20 to 35 percent of the population. In Latvia, where a large Russian community lives in the city of Riga, there is a strong movement to conduct official business in Latvian and to drop Russian language from school curricula. In Kazakhstan, Russians threaten to pull away from the Muslim Kazakhs, taking the northern regions with them. In Ukraine, where Russians are concentrated in the industrial eastern districts, the pro-Russian candidate failed to hold the presidency in November 2004 elections. Ukrainian nationalists clearly rejected falling back into Russia's sphere of influence.

Russians used to fill most of the best jobs everywhere in the USSR. Now, however, Russians typically find themselves out of favor in the non-Russian republics, where preferential hiring is common. In search of better opportunities, many ethnic Russians are leaving those republics and migrating to Russia. Between 1989 and 2002, 11 million people moved into Russia and 5 million left it, making Russia the world's third-greatest immigrant destination after the United States and Germany. This influx of migrants is welcome in Russia, where the population is shrinking by about one million people yearly. Immigration may also bolster Russia's labor force, which shrank from 85 million in 1993 to about 70 million in 2005.

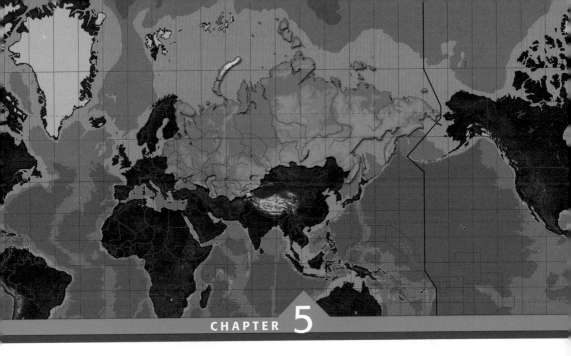

Cultural Geography

URBAN LIVING

Three-quarters of the population of Russia lives in cities. This is logical where winters are so long and cold. Whole groups of apartment buildings are commonly heated by a single community heating plant. There is no thermostat inside individual units, and the only way to relieve overheating is to open a window. Windows are all double paned, and doors have high sills to hold out drafts. Everyone has a heavy coat, a fur hat, mittens, and a scarf, and they bundle up thoroughly against the winter wind. Russians are generally quite fashion conscious—even when the temperature is −40°F (−40°C).

The average apartment is a crowded two-bedroom affair (the living room converts into a second bedroom) with a small kitchen,

A veteran of the Great Patriotic War (World War II), Fyodor Maslins and his wife, Ludmilla, live in a typically crowded apartment in the Russian city of Chelyabinsk.

water closet (bathroom), and a busy entryway. Some smaller apartments share a kitchen or bathroom among two or even three residents, but family apartments are usually more self-contained. Almost every family has a television and a refrigerator. Small shops are nearby, so city dwellers can stay as close to home as work and school will permit. Public transit by bus or subway is generally adequate in Russian cities, although winter cold and summer rains typically cast a grimy pall over urban commuting.

COUNTRY LIVING

The other 25 percent of Russia's people live in rural settings. Usually, people are gathered in a village of a few thousand, but there are also small hamlets of a few hundred. In Russia, almost no one lives on an isolated homestead as many American farmers do.

Most Russian villages are found in the European river valleys. Here, nobles of the eighteenth and nineteenth centuries ruled whole communities of serfs, or peasants, whose lives revolved around hard work and bare survival. In the twentieth century, lands of the nobility (and the peasant villages) were collectivized in service to the urban Industrial Revolution. The nobility was denounced, but the peasants were not really celebrated except in terms of their service to the military-industrial complex. Now, entering the twenty-first century, the peasant villages are still arranged for access to farmland, and the lifestyle there is still hard. It also is unhurried, family oriented, and self-reliant. The peasantry lives on in Russia.

Villagers' homes are generally freestanding wooden structures built of planks or logs. They are tightened against the winter and comfortable enough for families to spend long months in close proximity to each other and to the stove. The most important feature of the rural house is the private garden. Everyone grows tomatoes, beans, carrots, garlic, and potatoes. South of Moscow, melons and corn grow in private plots. Villagers still work on collective farms, although the farms are now officially called "privately owned" and the farm workers are even considered to be part owners. They still take direction from the farm manager, the harvest is turned in to the manager, and payments are decided and paid out by the manager. Private plots, however, belong to individual farmers, and the yields from these small gardens—up to one-half acre (.2 hectares)—are truly impressive. Rural Russians preserve their fruits and vegetables at home in glass jars, making them available throughout the year. Sometimes they trade produce for other necessities. They occasionally sell fruits and vegetables in the city, although transportation is difficult, especially in winter, when canned vegetables would earn a better price. They also fish and hunt small game. Many families own a cow, and goats are popular for milk and meat. Goats survive well in winter; they don't take much room, and they will eat anything.

Mud is a fact of Russian village life. This, combined with long distances between villages and cities, reduces Russians' mobility and commerce. Historically, therefore, Russian villagers have not traveled very much. This changed somewhat during the Soviet period, when cheap train and bus fares made trips possible. Roads are very poor, however, and travel has never been easy. Russia has fewer than 400,000 miles (650,000 kilometers) of road, most of which is gravel or dirt. The United States has more than ten times that much—nearly all of it paved.

Most Russians live in the western part of the country, where glacial till and peat mix into a soft surface. Summer afternoon showers keep paths and roads messy and full of puddles. Autumn brings one or two early snows that melt, turning the roads into deep mud until they freeze for the winter. Spring snowmelt practically erodes most roads all over the East European Plain, and the people grumble about their situation *bez dorozhye* (without roads). The road shortage probably saved them from annihilation in the Great Patriotic War, because the Nazis got lost going in and then found it almost impossible to get out. In the absence of personal transportation, however, it is almost impossible for rural Russians to improve their circumstances or to build businesses.

RUSSIAN SOCIETY

Russia is historically a patriarchal society. The father passes on his sense of dignity and pride in personal achievements. In place of a middle name, Russians bear their father's first name, typically followed by "-ovich" or "-evich" for boys and "-ova" or "-eva" for girls. Mothers, however, are the cohesive force in the family. They spoil their children and keep them as close as they can. This closeness has been reinforced, for as long as anyone can remember, by a serious housing shortage. Young people cannot move out before marriage and often remain in the home for a few years after they marry.

RELIGION

Throughout the Soviet era, religion was vigorously discouraged by the government, and few people risked their careers and benefits by attending church. The bulk of churchgoers were retired people, especially older women, and the true state of religion was a mystery. When the USSR collapsed, religion seemed to enjoy a spurt of growth in the early 1990s. The number of operating Orthodox churches in Russia grew from 3,000 in the 1980s to more than 11,000 in 1995. Everywhere in Russia, while the industrial economy was failing and the government struggled to attract foreign investment, church domes were being regilded. People with little to give nonetheless gave generously to restore Russian Orthodoxy to a leading position in society. Still, religion plays a puzzling role. For generations, it was all the peasants had against the brutish nobility, and it was a bedrock principle for great writers of the nineteenth century. About 40 percent of Russians now describe themselves as strong believers, and three-quarters of that group claims adherence to the Russian Orthodox faith. Religion was also eclipsed by a Soviet reverence for critical analysis, and the recent boom in church attendance still may not add up to a religious nation. Russian church attendance remains less than half that of the United States.

FOOD AND BEVERAGE

Russians drink black tea—coffee is gaining in popularity—and they like it sweet. They lodge a cube or a lump of sugar between their cheek and teeth and then filter the tea through it. This makes a tasty drink, but it also contributes to a high rate of tooth decay. Russians eat a lot of black rye bread, usually with butter or fruit preserves. Black bread is found everywhere and is baked fresh everyday. Americans love it. Cucumbers may be the most common food item in Russia. They are marinated, pickled, salted, sliced, chopped, and mixed with other vegetables, but they are almost always on the plate. Soups are also very popular, such as cabbage soup, pickle soup, fish soup, meat

The Soviet government actively discouraged the practice of religion. After the Soviet Union was dissolved, the number of Orthodox churches, such as this one in Moscow, rose from 3,000 in Russia in the 1980s to 11,000 in 1995.

soup, fat soup, and the delicious Russian *borscht* (red beet soup). Potatoes are a mainstay, and mineral water is usually on the table.

Most adult Russians drink vodka. A fine meal typically features it. A fancy Russian meal begins with so many tasty treats that it is hard to believe that bigger courses will follow. There may be caviar, egg salad, salami, strips of smoked salmon, salted herring, tomato salad, prepared mushrooms, cured cucumbers, and more. Every few morsels calls for a toast—be ready, you'll have to make one—and a shot of vodka. Periodically, everyone stands to talk, smoke, drink, and mill about. The courses keep coming. There are meat, fish, cutlets, soups, dumplings, *piroshki* (palm-sized meat, cheese, or vegetable pastries), salads, and wine, and it gets increasingly difficult to keep track of what is served over the next few hours. The company is warm, though, the food is wonderful, and the time flies by. At some point, everyone begins to sing. Welcome to Russia.

THE DACHA

Although most Russians live in cities, many urban families also maintain a summer cottage in the country called a *dacha*. The dacha is usually small, often cozy and comfortable, and practically always flanked by a garden. In a place of such long, hard winters, spring is a thrilling time. So it is with dacha owners, who busily work on their dachas and gardens every spring and deep into the summer. They grow vegetables and fruits and preserve what they can for the long, dark winter. Dacha building plots were often granted to union members or factory workers as part of a long list of benefits that came with the job. The nicest plots were granted to the factory managers, but everybody got his or her place in the sun. These days, many people buy dachas in rural villages that were depopulated as a result of industrialization, urbanization, bad roads, and now the rise of an urban service-based economy. For a culture where shopping and television were always only weak distractions, dachas became the national pastime. There is nothing odd about a subway rider in Moscow carting a good length of gutter on and off the train. It is for his dacha. Car owners have an advantage, of course, because the dachas and dacha villages are often miles beyond the last bus stop.

A NEW NATIONAL DIVIDE

Russians are typically and comfortably informal. As tough as times have been for them, there is a strong sense of shared sacrifice, and Russians rarely put on airs. "We're all in this together," they seem to say. There is "no sense pretending to be more or less than we are." Westerners, who are accustomed to people working their way up into higher society or richer surroundings, can be struck with how refreshingly honest and open Russian people are about their lives and their hopes for the future.

Despite this, it has suddenly become difficult to describe the average Russian. Under the Soviet Union, there was a tiny population of privileged elite and a huge majority of urban workers and rural peasants. The urban and rural lifestyles were distinct, but practically no one's material wealth stood out, and in neither place were there opportunities to get rich fast. Now, Communism is dead, and if capitalism hasn't taken its place, it has at least made a very public appearance. Russia is experiencing rapid transition; suddenly, there are a lot of people who got rich quickly. People are much more class conscious, and the gap between the "haves" and the "have nots" is more visible now than it was during the Soviet era.

The New Russians

Today, there is a new wealthy class, often called "New Russians." They are the ones who divided the spoils of, or otherwise positioned themselves, to benefit from the disintegration of the Soviet economy. These wealthy Muscovites—most of them are in Moscow—live in gleaming new luxury towers. Some of them also spend time in lavish new second homes (not to be confused with dachas). This group may be small in number, but its image is large. From Communist beginnings, these elite *biznismen* have amassed great wealth, and they show it. They buy expensive clothes and dine in fine restaurants. They socialize in chic health clubs and support one of the world's most successful Rolls Royce dealerships. Their children visit Brighton Beach (the site of a large Russian immigrant community) in Brooklyn, New York, just to see how Russian people used to live. Working for or around these super-rich biznismen are thousands of employees. Start-up companies are spinning off, and another wave of biznismen is emerging. They work hard, network, buy nicer apartments and foreign cars, and travel abroad. It should be noted, however, that life in Moscow is not typical Russia. In fact, no city—not even St. Petersburg—approaches Moscow in terms of power, influence, or wealth.

The "Lost" Russians

When we compare Moscow's nouveaux riche with the opposite end of the population, we see a much larger group of people, for whom the end of the USSR brought underemployment and the loss of a "social safety net." Under Communism, they were guaranteed free healthcare, free schools, vacations, and low prices for food, housing, and utilities. In mid-2003, it was reported that one-fourth of all Russian citizens and almost 70 percent of families with children lived near or below the poverty level of U.S. $67 per person per month.

A hospital bed is still free, but medicine is now terribly expensive for most Russians. Schools are still free, but their quality has lagged. Underpaid instructors sometimes even assign favors in exchange for grades.

Pensions are still paid to retirees but with important changes from Soviet days. Namely, they are more necessary now than before, but they are smaller in real terms. It is notable that, during the Soviet era, a government pension was only supposed to supplement private savings. The 1990s, however, brought a period of high inflation that wiped out the life savings of many workers who thought that they were comfortably prepared for retirement.

Russia has shown that an economy can be very delicate and that transitions must be carefully managed. During the Soviet era, the economy was state run and most of the country's population lived at a comparable socioeconomic level. Today's Russia faces many economic problems. It must develop a civil society, a strong middle class, and a strong business community in urban centers throughout the country. Classically educated

Many families in Russia must work hard to survive. This family with nine children lives primarily on the mother's pension. The father works on a collective farm, but does not expect to be paid until the new harvest.

professionals wonder how and where to direct their children. Families long sepeated by distant work and military assignments now contemplate the absence of opportunities. It is hard for young people to know what to do in regard to work or public service, or even what path to take in their personal lives. With meager pensions and savings often lost, elderly people were hardest hit by the post-Soviet displacement. Today, many can be seen selling their personal effects on the ground near the train station or making a little money sweeping streets with handmade brooms. Simply stated, a malaise has descended over Russia. Alcoholism is rampant and visible. People everywhere smoke heavily. The birthrate has dropped below the replacement level. There has been a dramatic rise in organized crime, and the country has been invaded by morally ambiguous or sexually suggestive advertising, fashion, music, and gangster style, mostly imported from the West. Sadly, the response to these changes has included a sharp increase in teenaged heroin addiction, gang violence, prostitution, and the transmission of *speed* (the Russian term for HIV). Gangsters are looked on with envy for their flashy night life, bodyguards, and blacked-out luxury vehicles. Crime is seen as an attractive alternative for some during times of economic and social uncertainty.

Living used to be much easier. The USSR provided a blueprint for a successful life. According to that model, talented children were channeled into intensive programs such as the arts or sciences, sports, the diplomatic corps, or other fields. Exceptional students became advanced engineers, entered the space program, won Olympic medals, or danced in world-class ballets. They also joined the Communist Party, where opportunities broadened. Less exceptional students were often assigned to trade schools. Many of these young people also went on to excel in their fields. Although their opportunities were limited, their futures were predictable. They could eventually get an apartment, raise a family, celebrate holidays, and otherwise take advantage of all of the cultural amenities that the socialist state provided. Many of those benefits are still available, even if they cost a little more. There are specially priced tickets to the symphony and ballet, and public transportation is still cheap inside the city. Families love to attend the circus, make regular visits to parks, and enjoy their dachas. They also travel to nature retreats the popular Black Sea resorts, though less frequently than they used to:

Meanwhile, the rich get richer. In 2001 and 2002, the richest 10 percent of Russians earned more than 40 percent of all national income while the poorest 10 percent earned less than 6 percent. Those who work in the new economy—banking, management, retail, telecommunications, accounting, languages, computers, and so forth—are poised to take even further advantage. Russian income taxes are low by European standards. Most Russians pay low rent by any developed country standard and they carry almost no debt. The wealthy elite—with their purchase of cars, homes, cellphones, kitchen makeovers, and designer clothes—may make a significant contribution toward regenerating the Russian economy. Retail sales are projected to nearly double between 2002 and 2008 to more than 200 billion dollars. Still, the growing gap between rich and poor is a bitter pill for most Russians to swallow.

Shopping

An interesting gauge of lifestyle is how people shop. A traditional Russian shopping trip is a time-consuming affair. The shopper stands in line at a certain counter in the food store (the meat, dairy, or canned goods counter, for instance) to find out what is available and how much it costs. Armed with this information, the shopper lines up at a cashier's counter to pay for the desired item—cash only, because no credit or debit cards are used. Then, receipt in hand, the shopper returns to the original product counter to exchange the receipt for the product. She puts her purchase in her bag—most food shopping is done by women—and moves on to another counter. This same system is found at the pharmacy, with different counters for medicines and tonics, bandages, and appliances.

Now, however, Western-style supermarkets are beginning to appear, especially in Moscow and St. Petersburg. Their shelves are stocked with imported goods, they have grocery carts, and credit cards are accepted. These modern stores are more expensive, and they usually demand hard foreign currency, which creates another economic irritant for Russian society. There is a new divide between people with *euros* or dollars and those with only Russian *rubles*. The ruble got a bad reputation for its withering slide during the 1990s. Most government workers and blue-collar laborers get paid in rubles, but suddenly, many white-collar workers hold foreign currencies. Cheap rubles make Russian exports more attractive in the global marketplace, but they also make Russians poorer. Holders of hard currency, on the other hand, see their money gain value in Russia, and they also invest in foreign banks whenever they can. This currency divide amounts to a security net for the new connected class, and it is a new source of widespread resentment.

A quicker way to shop is at a kiosk. A kiosk is a small stand with display windows that is towed onto a sidewalk. The owner buys goods of all types. Items for sale may include small toys, underwear, magazines, lottery tickets, ketchup, soft drinks, canned fish, and gum. There is chocolate and fruit juice, wine and flowers, and, of course cigarettes. The goods are marked up to a competitive level and sold. It is instant capitalism, and location is a key advantage in this blossoming form of capitalism. One good location can be near, or even inside, the pedestrian tunnels. These are the most popular (and only safe) way to cross the wide streets with speeding traffic that are common in most Russian cities. Within these wide passageways may be a lady selling flowers and a bookseller with a few tables set up. There may be elaborate glass booths stocked with cleaning products and snacks or even wholly enclosed metal structures selling clothing and cosmetics. They are open rain or shine, and they have a captive clientele of foot traffic. All of them, wherever they are on that busy street, pay for a "roof." This roof, however, is not protection from the rain. It is protection from the Mafia. Kiosk owners who fail to make a payment, or underpay, typically suffer physical violence or find their kiosk destroyed.

The Mafia

Russia's Mafia (organized crime) was operating by 1980, when consumer frustrations were climbing. At that time, while many store shelves were empty and consumer goods were so bad that

Street stands, or kiosks, such as this one offer an alternative to regular stores in Moscow. Items for sale include souvenirs, small toys, underwear, magazines, lottery tickets, ketchup, soft drinks, canned fish, fruit juice, and gum.

the leading cause of house fires was exploding television sets, mafia runners imported and distributed everyday luxuries like chewing gum and foreign cigarettes. The Russian government seemed unable to stop it. This trafficking intensified after the breakup of the USSR, when the collapsing economy dumped thousands of Red Army soldiers, secret policemen, and aimless young men into the labor market. Many lacked the skills for gainful employment, but they possessed the needed skills to threaten and hurt people. Russia's Mafia now numbers tens of thousands. It has developed global supply and distribution networks, and Mafia banks filter blood money into the world economy without detection. Every year, hundreds of people are killed by the Mafia. Most at risk are bankers who ask too many questions or businessmen who fail to pay them off and mend their "roof."

FOR WANT OF A CIVIL SOCIETY

In the United States and Western Europe, democracy is an established fact. Millions of people through many generations have joined organizations whose purpose is to uplift their communities and support their members. This voluntary, grassroots system is collectively called a "civil society," and is a rich cultural asset wherever it is found. It strengthens neighborhoods, brings people together, and both creates and sustains opportunities. Good works are the aim of fraternal and civic organizations such as the Elks, Lions, Shriners, Masons, Kiwanis, Rotary, and others. Charitable groups like the United Way, Salvation Army, Red Cross , and March of Dimes raise hundreds of millions of dollars for homeless shelters, summer camps, and medical research. Hospitals, recycling centers, soup kitchens, humane societies, and cleanup campaigns are staffed by legions of volunteers. Dozens of churches with hundreds of congregation members compete with each other to provide daycare, visit the sick, and counsel the troubled. Environmental organizations, labor unions, parent-teacher associations, farmer exchanges, scouts, collectors, historians, astronomers, gardeners, and many other groups spread goodwill and strengthen society. Very little of this exists in Russia.

Fundamental to the development of a civil society is a well-integrated infrastructure of transportation and telecommunications. Without it, people are frustrated in their efforts to network and cooperate. For example, in 2003, 58 percent of Americans had access to the Internet. Meanwhile, only 4 percent of Russians used the Internet. Today, barely 24 percent of Russians have personal access to a telephone. In the United States and Europe, telephone access is practically universal. Information is power. It makes communities stronger, businesses more responsive, and nations richer.

The civil society is an important component of what is often referred to as the "social safety net." In the United States and Europe, the social safety net is reinforced by layers of government programs. Hundreds of millions of people take comfort in knowing that their governments provide retirement assistance, protection from inflation, investment insurance, health and welfare assistance, and price controls on food and energy. All of these benefits were also delivered by the Soviet Union. Today, the most-watched measure for judging the Russian government is its ability to deliver a standard of living as good as the one that Russians remember under the USSR.

CHAPTER 6

Recent Political History

Nikita Khrushchev

After Stalin's death in 1953, the Communist Party leadership fell to a high-ranking group, but no individual could quickly build the mechanisms of terror and patronage with which Stalin had ruled absolutely. Shrewdly, Nikita Sergeevich Khrushchev muscled his way to the top of the Party. One of his methods was to popularize himself, and, in 1956, he took a big step in that direction. In February of that year, Khrushchev criticized the excesses of Stalin and promoted a wave of de-Stalinization in his so-called Secret Speech to the All-Union Congress.

    This Secret Speech was a watershed event and has been connected to the eventual opening up of the USSR. Khrushchev was energetic. He raised living standards for the Russian peasantry. Under the Virgin Lands Program, he ordered that new settlers plow up 80 million acres (32,400,000 hectares) of land—an area approximately the size of Arizona—and plant it with grain. He launched a vigorous foreign-relations campaign that ultimately made allies of many less-developed countries. At the same time, it was Khrushchev who presided over the great split between the USSR and the People's Republic of China. Also under Khrushchev, the USSR crushed a popular uprising against the Soviet-dominated government in Hungary. In the autumn of 1956, Hungarian farmers, students, and factory workers demonstrated for personal rights and freedoms that Khrushcev's Soviet Union simply would not allow. His response was swift and brutal, and more than 25,000 Hungarians died. The Cold War was heating up.

When the United States dropped an atomic bomb on Japan in 1945, the world was instantly convinced of thermonuclear power. The Soviets detonated their own atom and hydrogen bombs in 1949 and 1953, respectively. Next, they demonstrated ways to deliver them. Suddenly, there was a missile race that soon became a space race. In 1957, under Khrushchev, the USSR was the first to launch a series of earth-orbiting satellites, called Sputniks. In 1961, Russia became the first country to send a man into space. When Soviet missiles capable of reaching the United States appeared on the island of Cuba in fall 1962, the stage was set for a dramatic showdown between President John F. Kennedy and General Secretary Khrushchev. What came to be known as the Cuban Missile Crisis followed Kennedy's report to the nation that he would not stand for Soviet missile deployment so close to American soil. The world stood at the brink of nuclear war for a time, but Kennedy prevailed, and the missiles were removed. Khrushchev appeared weak, but he was not ineffective. In quiet negotiations, the United

Nikita Khrushchev makes a speech in 1962. Khrushchev became the leader of the Soviet Union after Joseph Stalin died in 1953. During the Cuban Missile Crisis, he and U.S. President John F. Kennedy squared off over the presence of Soviet nuclear arms in Cuba.

States agreed to remove its missiles deployed in Turkey. Still, Khrushchev's economic programs had not stimulated rapid growth and his raucous image was becoming an international scandal. By fall 1964, Khrushchev was retired from office.

Leonid Brezhnev

After Khrushchev's fall, Soviet leadership passed through a turbulent period before a new leader emerged in Leonid Ilyich Brezhnev. Brezhnev was born in 1906, so he hardly remembered a world before Stalin. He rose quickly through party ranks as Stalin ordered mass firings (and executions) of party and military officers above him. Brezhnev also was a favorite of Khrushchev. He had a sense of strongman rule, and he assumed it in his administration. Under Brezhnev, the KGB (the much-feared secret police) was strengthened. Soviet military power spread around the world, and the fight with China over leadership of the Communist world continued. The "Brezhnev Doctrine" asserted the Soviet Union's right to interfere with any Soviet-allied state, and he used it to invade Czechoslovakia in 1968 and Afghanistan in 1979. Brezhnev's hard-line credentials were clearly in order when he met President Richard Nixon, a man of firm anti-Communist convictions, in May 1972. Brezhnev and Nixon met against a backdrop of wars, intrigue, and the spread of deadly weapons. That meeting began a gradual de-escalation of tensions between these nuclear powers and a gradual normalization of talks between their leaders.

The USSR seemed like a vibrant place in those days. It attracted global attention for its political messages; the economy was predictable; the military was ominous; and political dissidents were gaining sympathy. That time is remembered favorably by many Russians today. Brezhnev's leadership was long, unchallenged, and secretive—traits not generally admired in a government. His term also coincided with the economic zenith and early decline of the USSR—a fact that Soviets managed to hide from the world for years to come.

Yuri Andropov

When Brezhnev died in 1982, another secretive transition process yielded another hard-line authority figure in Yuri

Vladimirivich Andropov. Andropov was affable, and he enjoyed Western culture—he even became the famous pen pal of an American schoolgirl. Andropov was still old-school, however. He had been the Soviet ambassador to Hungary when the USSR invaded that country in 1956, and for 15 years he served as head of the KGB. In 1983, his air force shot down a Korean Airlines passenger jet. The Soviet Union's assertive and military foreign policy rolled on. After a little more than a year in office, Andropov died.

Konstantin Chernenko

This time, the Moscow authorities appointed Konstantin Chernenko. Chernenko's political career had been spent writing propaganda—the art of convincing or scaring people into doing things for their country that they might not otherwise do. He wrote propaganda that condemned opponents of Stalin, and many of those people died. He promoted the government's highest decisions and ultimately attained its highest office—general secretary of the Communist Party. He died within a year.

Mikhail Gorbachev

When Mikhail Sergeevich Gorbachev rose to the Communist Party leadership in 1985, change was clearly on the way. Like Khrushchev, Gorbachev had served as minister of agriculture—always a weak point in the Soviet economy. Also like Khrushchev, Gorbachev was eager to shake up the system. Early in his term, the energetic and strikingly young Gorbachev initiated a program of economic *perestroika* (restructuring). He seemed to believe that the USSR could embrace efficiency in production, management, accounting, and government. This goal would be accomplished by retuning the existing Soviet command economy run by Gosplan, the goverment's central planning agency. At the same time, Gorbachev began to let factories and suppliers fail by withholding their government subsidies and exposing some of them to the dangers of a market rejection. In this way, he introduced elements of a parallel market system.

The Communist Party hard-liners around him warned that capitalism lurked in the hearts of biznismen. They cautioned Gorbachev that he was flirting with decentralization of Soviet power, which would weaken the privileged position of the Communist Party elite. General Secretary Gorbachev had seen the Soviet Union quickly become a world-leading producer of oil, steel, and wheat, however, and he saw it become a world leader in theoretical and applied sciences, a top builder of dams, ships, tractors, and perhaps even the strongest military power on Earth. He had lived through the Great Patriotic War, and he had faith that his great nation would rally one more time.

General Secretary Gorbachev even invited the people to speak out. *Glasnost* (openness) was a national call for citizens to criticize the quality of products, places of employment, public services, and even the leadership. It was also a promise that the government would respond. Freedom like this had never been attempted in the USSR. The initial reactions were favorable in Russia and generally more guarded in the other Soviet Republics. Russians in particular found their voices and entered into excited debate on street corners, on buses, on television, and in newspapers. Rather than inspiring change, however, glasnost inspired finger-pointing and generated a national consensus of gloom. It also awakened ethnic tensions across the Soviet Union and raised questions about the very legitimacy of the Soviet Communist Party. The first national semidemocratic election was held in 1989, but this served only to hasten the collapse of the system. That collapse came at the end of 1991.

Boris Yeltsin

Suddenly, instead of the USSR there were 15 new independent states. The Russian Federation emerged under the leadership of President Boris Yeltsin, who had been elected to his position in 1990, when Russia was still a part of the USSR. Yeltsin had distinguished himself through his opposition to the military's failed attempt to overthrow General Secretary Gorbachev in August

The first president of an independent Russia, Boris Yeltsin (center, speech in hand), makes a speech in front of the building of the Supreme Soviet of the Russian Federation in 1991. President Yeltsin held office until his retirement in 1999.

1991. Rather than supporting Gorbachev, however, President Yeltsin's protest was against the old Soviet axiom that stability comes at the point of a gun. The Russian people cheered him for it. This was the high point of his political career.

Vladimir Putin

President Yeltsin was elected for a four-year term in 1991 and reelected in 1996. He resigned at the end of 1999, turning over power to the most recent president, Vladimir Putin. Under President Putin, a more comfortable, if cautious, mood fell over the Russian economy. Buoyed by rising oil prices, the government's tax receipts rose and spending for public works, the military, and retirement pensions started to regain stability. President Putin was elected to terms in May 2000 and March 2004. His second and constitutionally final term expires in 2008.

THE DOWNFALL OF THE PRINCIPAL ADVERSARY

For most of the past century, Russia was the opposite of the United States in many ways. The government advocated Communism and led a world socialist movement, while the Western model pursued democracy and private property. The state-run economy stubbornly manufactured heavy machinery while Western companies diversified, computerized, and grew. The homeland was surrounded by still more land, while the West engaged in transoceanic trade in almost every direction.

Still, the Russian and American experiences have much in common. In both countries, pioneers crossed the wilderness, where wealth, adventure, and hardship ran unbroken to the great ocean thousands of miles away. In both cases, self-reliance was the settlers' code. Both peoples tested themselves against great forests, plains, rivers, and mountain ranges and gained confidence from the experience. Both nations confronted native peoples on their great transcontinental expansions, and, in each case, the natives lost. Both used their industrial power to develop huge militaries, and both practiced their systems on the world stage. The United States and Soviet Union were the principal competitors in the world.

Comparisons between the United States and USSR vanished in 1990, when the Soviet Union broke up. The world watched in disbelief when General Secretary Gorbachev read his resignation to the Soviet people. After that speech, the former general secretary sat for several minutes as if stunned. How could this have happened? Gorbachev (and Communist Party leaders in most of the other republic capitals) did not want this. Military leaders had tried to avoid it. The reasons are varied and subject to interpretation, but a short list can go a long way toward explaining what destroyed the USSR.

The Soviet Red Army Lost the Afghan War

It may be true that the USSR never threw its full weight against the Islamist mujahideen in the 1980s, and it probably is also true that the Red Army killed at least 100 men for every 1 they lost. The fact remains that the Soviets withdrew from Afghanistan with their objectives unmet and 13,000 fewer men. This failure weakened the public's faith in the military.

Polish Resistance Organized and Intensified

Since World War II, the USSR had maintained a political and economic "buffer zone" of control between itself and the democracies of Western Europe. However, the people of this area, which extended from Eastern Germany and Czechoslovakia in the north and southward to include Hungary, Romania, and Bulgaria, were overwhelmingly opposed to this arrangement. In 1980, the Solidarity trade union of Polish workers published a list of 21 demands, including freedom of speech and religion and improved working conditions. This event set the stage for a showdown over Soviet control of Central European "satellite states." The world watched as Soviet tanks massed for invasion at the Polish borders. The Poles were galvanized in their resistance by the ascension of Polish cardinal Karol Joseph Wojtyla to the Roman Catholic papacy as Pope John Paul II in 1979. The pope's campaigns for human rights brought world attention to the plight of the Poles and other nations colonized by the USSR. In 1989, the Communist leadership was swept from Poland, the Red Army did not invade, and a wave of democracy swept over the entire region. The Berlin Wall between East Germany and West Germany—a hated symbol of Soviet control—came down. Communist governments fell in Czechoslovakia, Hungary, and Romania. The Polish democracy movement ultimately freed Central Europe.

West Germany Practiced *Ostpolitik* (Eastern Policy)

In 1970, West German Chancellor Willie Brandt met with East German Willi Stoph. They discussed a final resolution of

World War II and the world's determination to keep Germany peaceful. At the same time, Chancellor Brandt worked to normalize relations with the USSR. In exchange for nonaggression and trade pacts (wanted by the Soviet Union), West Germany amplified its goals of reunion with East Germany and self-determination for all of Germany. Over the next few years, West Germany also opened dialogues with Communist Poland, Czechoslovakia, Hungary, and Bulgaria. Chancellor Brandt reasoned that talks would tear at the "iron curtain" that hung between the Western and Eastern communities.

This all amounted to a calculated risk. Some West Germans argued that to negotiate with East Germany was to legitimize the division of Germany. Ostpolitik did open borders between West Germany and the Soviet satellite states, however, and the differences shocked the Easterners. Soviet bloc economies were badly rundown by this time, and the poor quality of consumer goods condemned the system that produced them while exposing the lack of freedom needed to reform such a system. Ostpolitik was a not-so-subtle reminder that the whole Soviet empire was falling behind.

Japan's Economic Miracle Embarrassed the USSR

In 1950, per capita incomes were $9,573 in the United States, $2,834 in the USSR, and $1,873 in Japan. By 1973, however, per capita incomes were $16,607 in the United States, $11,017 in Japan, and $6,058 for the average Soviet citizen. Japan, with expanding capitalism, had leapfrogged over the socialist Soviet Union, and Stalin's vision for catching and overtaking the West was clearly discredited. Adding insult to injury, Japan did this with less than half the Soviet population, practically no natural resources, only 1.7 percent of the Soviet land area, and also having lost World War II. The Russians were on the winning side.

Western Militaries Spent the USSR into the Ground

Consecutive European and U.S. leaderships ordered and deployed expensive advanced weapons systems that the Soviets could not answer. Eighty percent of Soviet manufacturing was already military related; there was no room for redirecting assets. If the West was heavily burdened with preparations for another tank war in Europe, the Soviets were even more so. Finally, American President Reagan proposed and ordered the Strategic Defense Initiative, a multiyear, multibillion-dollar program that the Soviets could not match. The USSR was strategically outflanked.

The Soviet Economy Collapsed under Its Own Weight

Gosplan, the government's central planning agency, had failed to build a modern economy. The Soviet Union might have been the world's greatest steel producer, but manufacturing in Russia was hooked on orders and subsidies rather than on demand and competition. Factories thus produced goods as planned but not as needed. Gosplan juggled exchanges among millions of producers, suppliers, and distributors, without good computers telecommunications, accurate accounting, or market indicators that might tell people what anything was really worth. In the end, the Soviet economy collapsed under its own bureaucratic inefficiency.

It Was the Will of the People

Russians had their chance to defend a strong Soviet state when, in August 1991, a group of high-ranking Red Army officers took over the government and arrested President Gorbachev at his vacation retreat. They were overthrowing what they perceived to be a weak government and offering their own strong hand to steady the union's course. Never mind that all of the other forces of disintegration were in play; the people had found their voices now, and they soundly condemned the coup.

Even with all of this evidence, the Soviet breakup still shocked the world. Many asked, "Why didn't we see it coming?" The reasons vary, but they include the following. First, the USSR was a secret place. Its government did not broadcast its problems. Second, Western scholars and intelligence services were watching such a huge system that a total system failure might not have seemed possible. Finally, the world had faith in Soviet brutality. Past efforts to escape from the Soviet sphere of influence (East Germany in 1953, Poland and Hungary in 1956, Czechoslovakia in 1968) had met with such crushing force, that surely, it seemed, the USSR would save itself.

THE RUSSIAN POLITICAL SYSTEM

The new Russian constitution provides for a strong presidency and a weak legislature. The legislative branch of the Russian government consists of two bodies: the Federation Council and the Duma. The Council includes appointed members from all of Russia's 89 administrative units and is considered to be the upper house of the Russian Parliament. The Duma has 450 members directly elected by the people. It is the more contentious—even raucous—house of Parliament and is the place where partisan politics is most distinct. Duma representatives are elected to four-year terms. The 2003 elections cast strong legislative support to President Putin. In fact, those elections amounted to Russia's first clear political victory since the breakup of the USSR.

The judicial branch of the Russian government is led by the Constitutional Court, the Supreme Court, and the Superior Court of Arbitration. Judges for all of these courts are nominated by the president and then appointed to life terms by the Federation Council.

The current strong presidential situation is reminiscent of a system that elects individuals rather than a set of policies. Since 1991, Russia has witnessed a period of very weak party development. The rise and fall of political celebrities leaves the public

Current Russian President Vladimir Putin speaks during a 2005 meeting with members of the Russian Federation. As in the United States, the Russian presidency is limited to two terms of four years each. President Putin's second term expires in 2008.

yearning for a strong authority figure. Putin has been groomed for this role. His experience as a political operative and as a KGB officer seems to mesh with his inscrutable persona to keep his opponents off-guard.

President Yeltsin sought to weaken central control over Russia's economy by strengthening the federation of regional power centers. President Putin, on the other hand, has reversed that trend. In just a few years, he has rescinded Yeltsin's promise of greater autonomy to regional centers. Putin personally appoints regional governors; previously they were popularly elected. Putin also has lowered expectations of a free press. His government has harassed reporters, shut down television stations that broadcast unflattering stories about him, and ensured that his supporters control most of the media. He has intimidated and imprisoned wealthy businessmen who dared to challenge him. He has effectively eliminated opposing political parties. He has weakened the practice, begun under Gorbachev, of challenging leadership and has assumed the unquestioned political center of gravity in Russia. He even personally selected Russia's new national anthem.

The president is supported by his premier, or prime minister, who would assume the presidency if the president were forced to leave office, and by a Cabinet of Ministers. Each minister is responsible for managing a specific sector of government. There is also a Presidential Administration to assist in the day-to-day work of the presidency (drawing up documents, cross-checking with the constitution, and so forth) and a Security Council that reports to the president. All of these people are appointed by, and accountable to, the president.

As weak branches of government, the legislature and court systems could easily move closer to their old habits of simply approving whatever the chief executive wants. The public, too, seems relieved to have a strongman back at the helm. Corruption scandals have generally not implicated Putin, he has been helped by high oil prices, and he is not seen as too friendly, or compliant, with any foreign powers. Russians have generally favored his tough stand against the Chechens. His administration has paid pensions and wages on time, and his low-key, disciplined approach contrasts favorably with former President Yeltsin's sometimes clumsy personal style. Economic reform has gone ahead, and, after a disastrous decade, the economy is growing. Foreign investors are cautiously returning, and political life is still reasonably free by Russian standards.

Foreign Relations

Regarding foreign politics, Russia has been unable to resolve territorial disputes with Ukraine, China, Georgia, Estonia, and Latvia—ongoing issues that have existed since the time of the USSR. It also has yet to find a means of dividing mineral wealth under the Caspian Sea. A particularly thorny dispute involves either Russia's southern Kurile Islands or Japan's Northern Territories, depending on one's perspective. These four islands and their territorial waters were taken from Japan by the USSR in the last days of World War II, but they have significant Japanese histories. Their geographic position, however, ensures Russia's unimpeded access to Vladivostok—Russia's Far Eastern capital—and to the Sea of Okhotsk, a water body as big as Alaska. Return of these islands to Japan could also end World War II for both sides. It could also stimulate Japanese investment and do more for Russia's Far Eastern development than anything else could.

Russia's economy must also account for relations with Turkey. Relative to its size and the bulky nature of its exports, Russia has a serious lack of ports. From its Black Sea coastlines, Russia sends supertankers of oil to its favorite European markets. That is not a comfortable long-term arrangement for Turkey, whose great city of Istanbul hugs both shores of the treacherous Bosporus Strait—the narrow passage to the Mediterranean Sea. Relations between Russia and Turkey have been bad for centuries, and they remain just one tanker accident away from getting worse.

CHAPTER 7

Economic Geography

SOVIET RUSSIA

In 1928, General Secretary Stalin assigned the day-to-day running of his monumental industrialization campaign to Gosplan, the government's central planning agency. Its task was enormous. Raw materials were to be gathered and distributed, labor was to be trained and moved about, and managers and engineers assigned to hundreds of big projects—all at the same time. Gosplan spent 50 billion rubles on the first Five-Year Plan (1928–1933), 100 billion rubles on the second, and almost 200 billion on the third.

Gosplan's top-down management style was intended to serve political goals as much as economic ones. It made the USSR an industrial and military superpower in a remarkably short time, spread literacy across an illiterate nation, changed society from rural to urban, managed an industrial revolution, and collectivized agriculture. It did not perform with market efficiency, however, and the end result was a rigid industrial economy incapable of modernization. Gosplan and the central planning philosophy stayed at work until the end of the Soviet Union and perhaps even beyond.

INDEPENDENT RUSSIA

During the early post-Soviet days, there was a gradual dismantling of the state-controlled economy, and free-market opportunities appeared. Foreign businesses started to set up shop inside Russia. They were prepared to either make a lot of money in a wide-open, free-market economy or position themselves in advance of any government repossession of the economy. There were enormous transfers of wealth as government assets were selectively privatized. Remember, all assets belonged to the government. As privatization grew, government insiders gathered controlling interests in some of the most lucrative of these transfers.

Prices were released from government control in 1992; some food prices shot up to 12 times higher than they were. At the same time, the ruble was allowed to float relative to other world currencies, and it immediately started to lose value. Worried citizens looked for ways to protect their savings before those savings were simply lost to inflation. Many invested in capital growth (mutual) funds, but the biggest of these collapsed and investors lost everything. Visiting economic advisors from the West did not anticipate how dependent workers were on their old, inefficient state-run factories for schools, healthcare, stores, retirement, and more. When they advised President Yeltsin to "shut them down," the president cut off subsidies for whole industries. As a result, many failed because of their inability to compete unaided. Then the workers' social safety net, which was the greatest material benefit of living in the USSR, fell apart, too.

Boris Yeltsin was the first president of newly independent Russia, and his time in office naturally would be difficult. It turned out to be worse than most citizens expected. For ten years, marked by social despair and economic decline, he hung on to power. He dismissed government advisors as if looking for the right one with the key to turn Russia, the failing Communist state, into Russia, a winning capitalist one.

Unemployment

Gorbachev tinkered with the Soviet economy but failed to make it strong. President Yeltsin's tenure of chaotic marketization and confusing democratization caused a common gripe: "No more experiments!" Unemployment had spread from (officially) nothing to almost 10 percent of the work force. Youth unemployment (through age 25) hit 25 percent. Potentially worse is the very high and widespread level of underemployment now common throughout former Soviet society. In Russian cities, for example, factory workers and government bureaucrats frequently work only part-time or practically not at all. Still, however, they are employed, and they show up when the factories have work. This kind of activity is part of the "gray economy." For many workers, this is the prevailing economy, as they hustle work where they can and tend their dacha gardens closely. By the year 2000, Russians were generally tired of all this. They were losing faith in what they had come to think of as market democracy. Their cradle-to-grave pact with the government had weakened, and practically everyone was necessarily becoming more self reliant.

The Gray Economy

The gray economy involves trading in everything from stolen cars and military equipment to cigarettes and recreational drugs. Even innocent merchandise like food is traded "underground" because buyers and sellers can hide their transactions from tax collectors and save the money for themselves. Of course, their tax savings are eroded by payments for protection from the Mafia. Even government officials participate in the underground economy: In the early 2000s, Russians were paying 3 billion dollars and more every month just on bribes and "fees," mostly to government officials. The Soviet Union had a thoroughly state-run economy, and it was very hard to threw off that old bureaucracy.

Bartering is also a part of the gray economy, and all over the former USSR, people are good at it. As the value of Russia's currency, the ruble, dropped because of inflation in the 1990s, barter became a popular means of doing business. Bartering also kept business activity away from bank records, so neither the government nor the Mafia could easily find out who had what. Barter is impossible to measure, but, by 1998, it was thought to equal the entire rest of the economy.

For individuals, barter involves trading labor or personal possessions for money or something usable. Workers barter their labor for factory output or for deferred compensation—a vague promise of payment at a later time.

Between services and factories, barter involves the direct exchange of goods or services without money. Today, the practice has grown to include a huge web of credits and debits among suppliers, producers, and consuming firms. Barter is a terribly wasteful way of doing business. Traders are narrowly matched, firm managers occupy themselves with odd exchanges, and the unique terms of each deal make business unpredictable even after the deal is done. Buyers have power over sellers when they are issued credit on a handshake instead of with a legal contract. Sellers have to decide how much collection they will settle for when payment is due, and they may have to hire enforcers to hold that line.

For generations, Russians have operated shadow economies because a series of regimes denied them what they wanted or the means to get it. Arguably, Russians adjusted better in the 1900s, when their economy shrunk by half, than Americans did in the 1930s, when their economy shrunk by one-third. It would seem that the Russian workforce is remarkably adaptable. It is interesting to note that, although the Russian gross national income per person was $1,750 in 2003, the gross domestic product (GDP) per capita purchasing power parity (PPP—how much value that money apparently bought) was $8,900. The difference in part reflects the adaptable nature of the Russian people. In fact, reports at the end of 2003 that almost one-third of Russia's citizens were living below the poverty level might have been inflated.

Russia's inventive gray economy may turn out to have been a creative "bridge" between a mostly state-controlled economy and a mostly free one. Changes are afoot. By 2005, the government's reduction of subsidies to underperforming industries had made those industries' underreporting of profits no longer a lucrative act. Moreover, tax simplification and improved tax collection were lifting the official economy and shrinking the barter economy, especially counterproductive barter exchanges between industries. The amount of reform and growth in the Russian economy is hard to tell, however. Fifteen years of financial shifting off and on the books has had a caustic effect on economic statistics.

Current Trends

Charles Dickens might have called life in today's Russia "the best of times . . . the worst of times." At one end of society is a large segment of Russia's elderly population. For them, economic decline cut their pensions just when inflation ate up their savings. Now, beyond their earning years, they struggle. At the other end of society is a young cadre of professionals. Largely because of their success, the average Russian income has risen more than 12 percent annually since the turn of the century. The state of the Russian economy, it seems, is very much in the eye of the beholder.

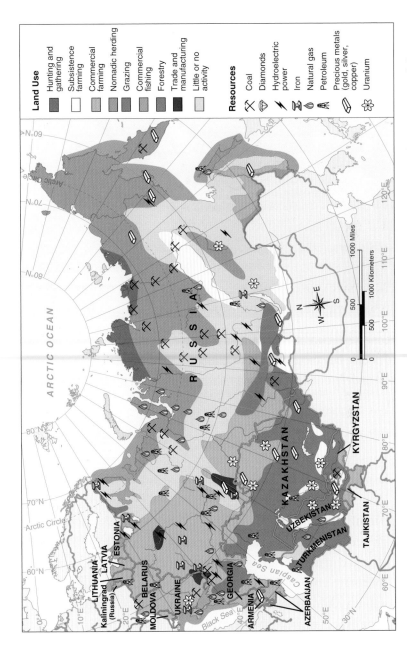

This is a land use map of Russia and the former Soviet republics. Oil plays a pivotal role in the economy of the countries in the southwestern part of this region. In the western nations, the people rely more heavily on agriculture.

Elderly pensioners sell cigarettes and vodka in downtown Moscow. Pensioners and unemployed people buy these items at wholesale markets and sell them at a higher price at underground stations and railway terminals in order to earn some extra money.

As the Russian economy moves through its second decade of transition, there is still widespread confusion about where it is headed. President Putin's stated goal is to establish a market economy, complete with rule of law, private property, and transparent markets (where costs and prices are widely known). Russia's economy still has many serious problems: Organized crime, official corruption, an old-thinking work force, and a shortage of corporate governance culture all hinder economic growth and stability. Add to this an exodus of many trained professionals, a huge export of wealth, and ugly nationalist politics, and it is little wonder that many foreign firms are discouraged from investing there, even in Russian's huge mineral and energy reserves. Clearly, growing the Russian economy will take some time.

LIVING OFF THE LAND

By far, the greatest engine of Russia's economy is the export of raw materials. The country has vast stores of gold and other metals, timber, and especially oil and natural gas. Sale of these commodities accounts for 85 percent of exports by value and the biggest part of Russia's GDP (gross domestic product).

Minerals

Russia has rich mineral deposits. It is a world leader in the production of beryllium, asbestos, gold, diamonds, iron ore, nickel, platinum, and tin, and it still has vast tracts of unknown resource wealth. Unfortunately, many of these mineral deposits are in remote locations, and Russia's shrinking work force does not produce enough mineral-industry workers who are willing to live in hostile environments. Therefore, Russia's mineral wealth will continue to reveal itself slowly. It also will probably gain value as the world's other, more easily exploited supplies become depleted.

Timber

Russia has the world's largest forests. Since the republics became independent, privatization has put most of Russia's forests in the care of private companies or groups with foreign investment. At the same time, weakened state controls have allowed black-market timber to leave the country at an alarming rate. Russian mills process far less domestic timber than do most other wood-exporting countries. Employment in this industry is therefore less than it could be. In fact, Russians often must reimport their own wood from Finland and other nearby countries in the form of paper and wood-based products.

Agriculture

Russian agriculture, which employs almost one-fifth of the labor force, suffers from the same disincentives that plagued Soviet-era farmers: absence of clear ownership, absence of

Pictured here is an oil refinery of the YUKOS oil company. The oil industry is vital to the Russian economy. Estimates put Russia's oil reserves second behind only Saudi Arabia's.

markets and suppliers, and absence of a strong food-processing industry. Until these problems are solved, the government will continue to subsidize farming and Russia will remain a net importer of food. Russia's fishing industry also has not yet completed its transition from the Soviet system, and processed-fish imports have grown significantly in recent years.

Machinery

Heavy machinery was a main product of Soviet industry. Designs were not innovative, but durability was generally good. Now, the energy sector is a prime consumer of machinery and orders are up. Added to that is the high priority government attaches to public transportation and Russia's 4-billion dollar arms export business. There are also 800 million dollars in nuclear technology exports and 500 million dollars in ship sales. These factors, combined with increased investments in production during recent years, suggest that future prospects for Russian industry are good.

Oil and Natural Gas

Russia's best-performing industry is oil. The country has a lot of oil, with estimates of proven crude-oil reserves that run as high as 150 billion barrels. If true, this resource puts Russia in second place behind Saudi Arabia, with 260 billion barrels, and ahead of Iraq, with 115 billion barrels. Russia is also the world's richest country in natural gas; the largest known gas fields are in the Western Siberian Lowlands. In fact, just this one basin is estimated to contain more gas than the total second-place reserves of the United States.

The oil business, however, is cyclical; this is particularly true in the case of Russia. In the late 1980s, Soviet output of hydrocarbons (oil and natural gas) was the world's highest, hitting 12 million barrels per day. Throughout the 1980s, the USSR laid twice the length of the Alaskan Pipeline every year. Then, technical and management problems resulted in a long period of decline, to about 7 million barrels per day in 2002. Russian production is now beginning to climb again and is widely expected to reach 9 to 10 million barrels per day in the near future. This level of production should be sustainable for the next 30 years or so.

Russia's economic health clearly is tied to the price of oil. In 1997, oil prices headed downward and Russia's tax collections fell. In October 1998, the government failed to make payments on its enormous foreign debt. Foreign investment stopped, and the Russian economy nearly collapsed. Oil prices soon rose again, and the economy started to recover in 1999. Certainly, the low value of the Russian ruble made Russian exports cheaper, and the October 1998 default forced the government to make deep cuts in spending. Oil and gas exports provide half of Russia's government revenue. In 1998, a one-dollar-per-barrel oil price increase brought in almost one billion dollars in extra government earnings. This number is significant, considering the entire federal budget that year was 59 billion dollars.

Since 2000, Russia has benefited greatly from a quadrupling of world oil prices. In recent years, Russia has amassed large trade surpluses, so that, by 2005, it had 200 billion dollars of hard-currency reserves. This situation has enabled Russia to shrink its foreign debt, increase its credit rating, generate an air of stability, and stimulate foreign investments. It also makes Russia a new and rising political player in the world capital market. Suddenly, investments from Russia into euro- or dollar-denominated accounts can nudge the value of those foreign instruments up or down. This is new.

Fortunes are made from Russian oil and gas. By 2001, only a decade after the republics became independent, Russia had eight billionaires. At least five of them acquired their wealth selling oil and gas. These people have power, and it is not controlled by the government. This was a first in living memory, and it forces a showdown. Consider this: In 2004, the Russian government seized the assets of the oil company YUKOS and arrested its chairman on tax-evasion charges. This action alone firmed up world oil prices, and that would be good for Russia. It also can have a chilling effect on all big business activity in Russia, because YUKOS is big. It pumps and sells 1.7 million barrels per day, more than the entire production of Libya. If the government can shut down YUKOS, it can shut down anybody. More important, YUKOS's chairman is a political opponent of President Putin. Businesspeople everywhere can remember when the USSR suffered from Communist Party control. Now, those same people—when wondering where to build a factory or buy a commodity—are forced to consider that Russia could slip back toward more state control. For success, business needs a system of predictable and transparent law, not erratic men.

Crafty Russian entrepreneurs will continue to amass fortunes as long as energy prices are high and accounting practices are lax. The exploitation of natural resources, however, by nature, concentrates decisions in the hands of a few people. The true wealth and power of an elite few individuals may never be known. Just as predictably, great numbers of Russians will never work in the oil industry. It is true that commodity sales enhance Russian tax collections. This may be an attractive outcome to children of the USSR, who were raised on the idea that price controls, jobs, housing, and practically all social benefits come from the state. An oil-based economy, however, will not spread wealth or the means of generating wealth to the population at large.

It is also notable that Russia's grip on Chechnya involves oil—both under the land and crossing over it. The Caspian seabed is a huge source of oil, and Azerbaijan moves a fortune in it over Chechnya on its way to tankers at the Russian Black Sea port of Novorossiysk. This is an important Russian moneymaker. It also ties into an anticipated growth in oil traffic from Kazakhstan, and the Russians are intent on holding this business. Quiet in the North Caucasus region is something that Russia wants dearly. It is ironic, however, that, at least for the short term, political instability and even war in close proximity to Russia could serve Russia's interests: Conflicts around the Caspian Sea and the Persian Gulf involve the capture and delivery of oil, and when oil is threatened it becomes more valuable.

CONCLUSION

The economy is working well for some Russians, and this economic success has a ripple effect for many others in Russian society. Every year since the 1998 default, the economy has grown. Most of the best-paying jobs and much of Russia's current prosperity are in the service sector, which did not even exist during the Soviet era. It is an interesting contrast to see old communist wall murals near modern Moscow storefronts, where rents can approach $250,000 per year. Capitalism has taken root here very rapidly.

The average Russian, however, does not trade shares in companies or hide profits in vague investments like kiosks or candy companies. She doesn't shop in the expensive fashion boutiques with hard currency, and he doesn't drive a foreign car. Most Russians do not know what to make of the new economic "system." They are, however, a sharing people, and they will generally share their opinions on the topic. The question, "Is this capitalism?" will generally be answered, "It must be, since so many young men seem to be getting rich." "Is this socialism?" "Yes," they say, "but it still is a weak substitute" for the cradle-to-grave security they used to enjoy. "Is this a dictatorship?" "No," they say. They can remember that, and this is not it.

CHAPTER 8

New Countries on the World Scene

Russia may have been the biggest and most powerful of all the Soviet republics, but it was only 1 of 15. The other 14 are also independent states now, reforming themselves or reforming their presentations of themselves. Most of them banded together politically in the wake of the Soviet breakup. That loose association was called "the Commonwealth of Independent States" (CIS). The CIS was a natural bridge from union to separation. In fact, the former Soviet republics were not truly separate for some time. Their infrastructures—telecommunications, pipelines, railroads, and air routes—were tightly integrated, and their monetary policies (regulation of money supplies and interest rates and even their currencies for a time) also were tied together. Their populations were mixed, with Russians in non-Russian republics and with non-Russian nationals in Russia and to a lesser extent scattered throughout the other republics. A marriage of 70 years, whether happy or not, would not dissolve easily.

Like its many counterparts elsewhere in the world, the CIS established its own common economic space. Within the commonwealth, capital, products, and people might move to where they are most needed and most profitable. A free-trade zone works only where the forces of attraction outweigh the benefits of separation, however, and through the 1990s, CIS economies did not perform as well as those of Europe, South Asia, or most of East Asia. Even Russia has been drawn away from its own trade zone by the lure of healthier and wealthier customers. Russian exports to the other former republics now account for less than one-fourth of the country's total. Exports to the European Union, on the other hand, amount to about 60 percent of Russia's total international sales. By summer 2004, President Putin was calling for a rededication to the CIS, "or this structure will be washed away from the geopolitical space."

In Russia, there is such a close association with the old empire that the common reference to non-Russian former republics is "near-abroad," as compared with the truly foreign countries, called "far-abroad." That feeling is not matched in the "near-abroad." Some of these countries have been affiliated with Russia for less than a century and others for more than 1,000 years. All of them are looking outward now, building new foreign relations, and, in some cases, reexamining old ones. The end of CIS would distance these republics even further.

THE BALTIC STATES

Northwest of Russia, facing Scandinavia and hugging the Baltic Sea, are Estonia, Latvia, and Lithuania. These three states were independent between the two World Wars, but they all landed in the Soviet sphere of influence as a result of the Hitler-Stalin Pact of 1939 (which divided most of Central Europe between Germany and the USSR) and were made Soviet republics in 1940.

This imperial act was deeply resented by the Baltic peoples, and it was never recognized by the United States. The Baltic States were the first republics to leave the USSR in September 1991.

In language, religion, and culture, the Baltic nations have always been closer to Western Europe and Poland than to Russia. Affirming this fact, they all joined the European Union in 1994. This political shift westward, together with efforts to elevate native languages to superior official positions, presents a cultural problem for the large Russian minorities (about 30 percent) in Estonia and Latvia. The Baltic hope is that closer ties with Europe will protect them, but political independence next door to mighty Russia is always subject to change.

BELARUS

Belarus (White Russia) is a flat-to-rolling, Kansas-sized country of 10 million people sandwiched between the domineering cultures of Poland, Ukraine, and Russia. Belarus is landlocked and is separated from its big southern neighbor, Ukraine, by sprawling swamplands. Its rivers flow outward to the north, west, and south, but none of them serves to integrate the country. Marshes have been drained for more than a century, and today about one-third of the country is farmed on "reclaimed" land.

Belarus has been the primary victim of the April 1986 explosion and fire at the Chernobyl nuclear reactor in Ukraine. Thirty-five tons of radioactive debris (70 percent of the total) settled over the southeastern quarter of Belarus, forcing whole towns to evacuate and sending cancer rates soaring. According to government figures, Belarus sustained U.S. $235 billion dollars in damages from the Chernobyl accident, roughly ten times the country's annual gross national product (GNP). It is believed that 20 percent of the population has suffered dislocation or sickness from Chernobyl, and the birthrate in Belarus has fallen by half. This is a huge long-term disaster.

Belarus was one of the more prosperous republics under the Soviet Union, and its capital, Minsk, is where the CIS was formed. Its government is unapologetic about maintaining control over the press, the courts, political opposition, and business in general. Belarus has strong rail and pipeline connections with Russia, most of its industrial exports go to Russia, and energy imports come from there. It was heavily "Russified" during the Soviet period, and today Russian is the most commonly spoken language in the cities. A popular movement even calls for reintegration with Russia. This is not the political trend in either the Baltic States or Ukraine, so Belarus is rather isolated in the region for its attraction eastward.

UKRAINE

The second-largest and most powerful of all of the non-Russian republics was Ukraine, a country almost as large as France. Ukraine was the industrial anchor of the Soviet Union and produced huge percentages of Soviet coal, iron, and steel. Adequate moisture and broad expanses of flat land make Ukraine ideal for growing grain, and the country was appropriately known as the USSR's "breadbasket." Its soil is so dark and rich that, when the Nazis were retreating westward across Ukraine in the closing days of World War II, they took trainloads of it back to Germany.

Ukraine also has a place in Russian hearts for the central role that Kiev played in the rise of Russia. For this reason, and for the way subsequent empires have relied on Ukraine's natural resources, Ukrainian independence has been hard won. After the Russian empire fell, Ukraine asserted its independence in 1918 but lost it to the Communists in 1922. "To lose Ukraine," wrote V.I. Lenin, "would be to lose our head." The interwar years were a disaster for Soviet Ukraine. Collectivization of farmlands resulted in a famine which killed 6 million Ukrainians. When World War II practically destroyed Ukraine and the rest of the western USSR, it briefly looked as though a sovereign Ukraine might rise from the ashes. Stalin reimposed Soviet tyranny with a vengeance, however, and independence did not return to Ukraine until 1991.

Ukraine's key opposition leader, Viktor Yushchenko, takes the oath of office in parliament. Yushchenko was declared the winner of a disputed presidential election in November 2004.

In November 2004, Ukrainian citizens elected a president who has vowed to move the country closer to Europe economically, culturally, and even militarily. The unspoken message is that Ukraine also will move farther from Russia. From the standpoint of Russian "Eurasianist" thinkers, who see Russia as a center of influence rather than at the margins, this is not in Russia's interests. These Russians, led by President Putin, endorsed the incumbent prime minister for the job, and for a time, it looked as though the old Communist Party machine would activate that transfer of power. Then came the election. As predicted, the declared winner was Prime Minister Viktor

Yanukovich. However, the ballot tampering was so blatant and the crowds of protestors so large, that the government was forced to have a runoff. This time, the opponent, Viktor Yushchenko, won. There is excitement, especially among young Ukrainians, over the prospect that, this time, Russia really has lost Ukraine.

MOLDOVA

Between southwestern Ukraine and Romania is the former Soviet Republic of Moldova. It is practically framed by rivers, with the Prut on its western frontier with Romania and the Dniester running roughly parallel to its eastern border with Ukraine. Moldova's climate is mild, its soils are good, its water supply is adequate, and its topography is manageable. For the Soviet empire, Moldova had that rarest of riches—heat. From this subtropical republic come fruits and melons, corn and beans, vegetables, nuts, flowers, and world-class wines.

Although Moldova is practically framed by rivers, east of the Dniester is a strip of the country's richest land that Moldova does not control. When Moldova gained independence in 1991, a sizeable Slavic population and an entire division of the Russian Soviet army was stationed in Transdniester, this ribbon of land across the river. These Russians have decided not only to remain there, but they also declared Transdniester independent of Moldova in 1992. There is not much that Moldova can do about this. From its capital, Chisinau, the government has appealed abroad for support. Unfortunately, there is not much that the international community can do about the situation either, at least for now.

Another semi-independent region is Gagauz, in southern Moldova. In a peaceful process, the Christianized Turkish Gagauz people gained autonomy for themselves in 1994 while still respecting Moldovan sovereignty. This development is significant. It is the first of its kind in Europe, where many countries contain large ethnic minorities.

Moldova is no stranger to foreign takeovers. For 3,000 years, the area was alternately controlled by Dacians, Greeks, Romans and Vlachs, Huns, Ottomans, Magyars, and the Golden Horde (the Mongol Empire in Russia). Emerging from a single principality, Moldova began in the fourteenth century. Turks and Russians fought over it for most of the eighteenth century. The Russians held it, then Romania, and then the USSR after the Great Patriotic War. Moldovans were (and still are, ethnically and linguistically) akin to Romanians, but that connection was interrupted by the Soviet takeover in 1940. Thereafter, Soviet policy was to convince Moldovans that they were not Romanian but a distinct people closely related to the Ukrainians and Russians. Parents risked lengthy prison sentences for teaching their children otherwise. The border was closed, history books were rewritten, the language was altered, the Romanian alphabet (which is Latin, like the English alphabet) was replaced with the Eastern Slavic Cyrillic alphabet. The propaganda wave of Russification struck hard in Moldova. Moldova's continued independence may ultimately give way to a reunion with Romania, but not anytime soon. In 1994, Moldovans voted overwhelmingly to remain independent.

INDEPENDENT STATES OF THE CAUCASUS REGION
Georgia

On the southern flanks of the Greater Caucasus Mountains, the country of Georgia descends from snow-capped peaks, across a wide band of foothills, into a broad subtropical river basin. Georgia's physical landscape is so complex that a wide variety of microclimates supports a diverse agriculture. Crops include hearty grains such as barley and oats, wheat and corn, wine grapes and peaches, nuts, tea, tobacco, and even citrus fruits. Orange groves of the Rioni River Valley made Georgia a particularly valuable province of the Soviet Union. The Black Sea coastline is beautiful and famous for its sunny

The growth of Georgia's economy depends on the oil industry. Petrotrans Limited, pictured here, transports crude oil and refined products from Gardabani, in eastern Georgia, to Batumi, in western Georgia, by way of the Black Sea, near the Turkish border.

resorts and long-lived people. Georgia is a picturesque destination, especially for vacationers from the cold north.

Because of its location next to and between great powers, Georgia has been the historic possession of Romans, Armenians, Arabs, Mongols, Turks, Persians, and, most recently, Russians. Today, Georgia is home to 100 different ethnic groups, and three strong-willed minorities have practically removed their territories from Georgian control.

Independence came before Georgia was ready for it. The process of economic reform has been complicated by Russia's desire to maintain exclusive trade ties with Georgia and keep military bases there. Lying between the oil-rich countries of the Caspian Sea and energy-poor Turkey may give Georgia an opportunity to improve its own energy security. Big foreign-financed pipeline projects are planned to cross the country.

In November 2003, Georgia essentially had a revolution. President Eduard Shevardnadze suddenly resigned after a tumultuous and discredited election, and opposition leader Mikhail Saakashvili swept to power. Shevardnadze had been the last foreign minister of the USSR and enjoyed international popularity for his role in the demise of the Soviet Union. Georgia, however, suffered under his presidency. Economic development decreased, employment collapsed, and his administration was widely regarded as corrupt. The average wage was about one dollar per day, and pensioners received far less than that. Saakashvili inspired a peaceful transition, and he hopes to maintain close and stable relations with both Russia and the United States. However, Georgia also demonstrates the danger lurking for first-generation, post-Soviet governments with wasted economies, weak civil societies, and no tradition of orderly democratic succession.

Armenia

Present-day Armenia is only a small remnant of the ancient Armenian Empire that once included parts of the Black Sea and even Mediterranean Sea shorelines. Centuries of invasion have left Armenia landlocked and extremely isolated, however. Armenians have been brutally persecuted by their western neighbors, the Turks, and they are at war with their eastern neighbors, the Azeris. Armenian Orthodoxy was the world's first Christian church. Their most helpful trading partner, however, is the Islamic theocracy of Iran, which sells them natural gas. Armenia's most treasured national symbol, Mount Ararat, now stands on the other side of its closed border with Turkey. Today, only about a quarter of all ethnic Armenians live in Armenia.

Ninety-seven percent of Armenia's population is ethnic Armenian. They have formed a strong and educated nation in this difficult natural and political setting. Armenian technology was some of the best in the USSR, but its customer base and energy suppliers dried up with the end of the communist state. Arable land is limited in Armenia, and rainfall is scarce. A devastating earthquake hit in late 1988, killing 25,000 people and revealing the inadequacy of Soviet construction techniques. The nuclear power plant at Metsamor has been called unsafe since the 1988 quake, but the government cannot afford to close it. Armenia is lacking in energy resources, so expanding natural gas deliveries from Iran makes economic sense for both sides. Today, Armenia's biggest supporter is the United States. The United States, however, is wary of Armenia's increased dependence on Iran.

Azerbaijan

Azeris are a Turkish people, but they are separated from Turkey by their archenemy, Armenia. Azeris are Shiite Muslims, like Iranians to the south, and there are twice as many Azeris in Iran as there are in Azerbaijan. The language barrier between these two nations is formidable, however. Early in the Soviet era, some odd border decisions placed a large Azeri region to the southwest of Armenia and a large colony of Armenians inside Azerbaijan. That colony is called Nagorno Karabakh. Independent Armenia wants it back, and its forces have occupied it. In 1994, a cease-fire was enacted. Still, Armenia occupies 20 percent of Azerbaijan, and one million people are refugees from that conflict.

Azerbaijan has tremendous oil wealth. Until the twentieth century, it was the most important oil-producing land in the world. Today, oil generates 70 percent of the national export income, yet Azeris remain desperately poor. Now, with foreign investments, there is hope for an economic turnaround. Azerbaijan's state-owned oil company has closed deals with energy giants Amoco-BP, Exxon, and Unocal, among others. These alliances could raise more than 50 billion dollars in development funding for the country. Azerbaijan still will be isolated from the world ocean, however, and an alternate pipeline network is needed to complement the present route that is provided, and controlled, by Russia.

Today, Azerbaijan's government remains an elitist institution. Few Azeris feel connected to their government. Great wealth concentrates around the privileged leadership. Terrible oil spills have destroyed much of Azerbaijan's Caspian coastline, and chemical pesticides have been carelessly used on farmlands. Not much is being done to correct these problems. Fortunately, almost one-third of Azeris farm, so subsistence agriculture (Azerbaijan has as many goats and sheep as it does people) and small-scale exchange relieve the government of high public expectations. Unfortunately, substantial tracts of good farmland are currently closed by the Nagorno Karabakh conflict.

INDEPENDENT STATES OF THE OLD TURKISTAN

East of the Caspian Sea and south of Russia are the five Islamic states of Central Asia. These lands, whose names all end with *-istan* ("land of"), were invaded by Persians 2,000 years ago, settled by Mongols 800 years ago, and conquered by Russians a century ago. The people of Central Asia were generally displeased with their status within the USSR, but their Communist Party leaderships were comfortable enough with the old bureaucratic system that they have, for the most part, kept centralized political and economic controls in place, as well as their own privileged positions.

Together, these newly independent countries were known for centuries as West Turkistan. The area included a network of tribes—some nomadic and others settled—whose place between several great empires made them attractive for conquest. Situated between Rome and China, for 1,000 years they lay on the Great Silk Road. Later, thanks to their location between Russia and British India, they could tilt the global balance of power from the continental interior outward or from the maritime trading world inward. Soviet planners created five republics out of this land in order to isolate some tribes and to divide others. Today, these Central Asian countries again lie at the center of great controversies.

Kazakhstan

On the eastern shore of the Caspian Sea lies another oil-rich state, Kazakhstan. Like Azerbaijan, landlocked Kazakhstan faces a serious challenge in moving its oil to market. Currently, Russia transports most of it, but other routes are possible. Wherever it moves—into China, across Afghanistan and Pakistan, across Iran to the Persian Gulf, or over Russia to the Black Sea—Kazakhstan's oil will energize development and strengthen political relations. Very little commerce moved into Central Asia during the last two centuries. There is a lot at stake in Central Asia's turning outward now.

Tribes matter in Kazakhstan, where family is the social safety net and whole villages and professions can involve a single clan. The rural and storytelling traditions still live here, and listening and conversing are national pastimes. Traditionally, Kazakhs were a nomadic people. They kept goats, camels, cattle, and horses. Some still do. Their migratory ways, together with their primary social structure, were all upset with their forced assignment to Soviet-style collective farms between 1926 and 1937. This was resisted both secretly and violently, but collectivization was implemented nonetheless. Nomads became grain farmers, farmers moved into village apartment blocks, children went to school, industrialization occurred, and modern cities grew. This process, however, resulted in the death of one-quarter of all Kazakhs.

Another element of sovietization in Kazakhstan was the coerced and induced inflow of non-Kazakhs. Today, Slavs and even some Germans account for 40 percent of Kazakhstan's 15 million people. This ethnic imbalance keeps the country in suspense, as does the ethnic Russians' constant grumbling about seceding from Kazakhstan and taking their mineral-rich northern provinces with them. Only about 44 percent of the population speaks Kazakh. National identity thus remains a delicate subject in Kazakhstan.

A more practical problem is that Kazakhstan is polluted. Farmlands in the south have been salinized by excessive irrigation. (Salinization occurs when surface water evaporates in the extreme heat and the soil minerals form a toxic crust on the surface.) To the west, the Aral Sea has practically starved to death because of the diversion of water from the Amu Dar'ya and Syr Dar'ya rivers for irrigation purposes. Eastern Kazakhstan was used as a testing range for more than 500 aboveground nuclear explosions. Radiation levels remain dangerously high.

Despite its top-heavy energy sector, Kazakhstan has a reasonable chance of developing a balanced economy. It has an enormous grain-growing area; there are well-integrated mining, steel-making, and industrial manufacturing centers; and it is home to perhaps the world's busiest spaceport at Baikonur.

Kyrgyzstan

Kyrgyzstan's Nebraska-sized territory is 93 percent mountainous, but most of the country's 5 million people live in its three valleys. Its people are agrarian and traditionally nomadic, herding their flocks upslope in spring and downslope in fall. Kyrgyzstan has twice as many sheep as people. The country also has sizeable uranium deposits, large gold reserves, plentiful freshwater, and a major potential tourist attraction in pristine alpine Issyk-Kul (High Lake).

Kyrgyzstan, like Kazakhstan, grapples with significant minority populations. With 14 percent of the population ethnically identified with its big neighbor, Uzbekistan, and another 20 percent being Russian Orthodox, policies here cannot comfortably advocate for the Kyrgyz people. Its wealth of mountain snowmelt, for example, has been largely dammed to benefit agriculture in neighboring Uzbekistan. Its borders are made up of several exclaves, or "islands," of Uzbek territory inside Kyrgyzstan. This wasn't a problem in the Soviet Union, when nationalism among tribes was less of an issue. It is a big issue now.

Kyrgyzstan's president, Askar Akaev, was unique among Central Asian leaders. He rose to power as a reformer rather than from the ranks of Communist Party officials. In the early 1990s, President Akaev charmed international agencies with his commitments to economic reform and his warm words about democracy. The economy, however, became dismal. Health-care declined, inflation ran at 95 percent annually through the 1990s, and two-thirds of the population fell below the poverty line. The average annual income is a paltry $330.

In the spring 2000 elections, President Akaev's supporters won a large number of the parliamentary seats. Election fraud was charged by his opponents and by foreign observers, as well. Akaev's international popularity slipped. In May 2002, President Akaev ceded 327 square miles (847 square kilometers) of disputed territory to China, and this provoked mass protests. Akaev claimed that this was the best deal he could get. Still, his credibility was damaged and his support was dwindling. The economy was stagnant, yet rumors spread about the president's accumulating wealth. His children had become rising political stars, censorship was increasing, and opposition candidates languished in jail.

In March 2005, new elections were again widely criticized as corrupt. This time, however, Kyrgyzstan suffered a sudden and violent overthrow of the government by a loose collection of dissidents called the People's Movement of Kyrgyzstan. President Akaev disappeared, and the capital, Bishkek, was wracked by looting and strong-arm robberies. This was the third recent revolution in a former Soviet Republic, following overthrows in Georgia (2003) and Ukraine (2004). Kyrgyzstan's coup-d-etat, however, is perhaps more worrisome because it lacks a clear message or spokesman. Political chaos is an incendiary condition.

Uzbekistan

Uzbekistan is the Central Asian anchor. With 27 million people, it outnumbers all of its neighboring countries combined. It is the leading agricultural producer in a mainly agrarian part of the world. Uzbekistan contains the region's greatest concentration of historic and cultural sites, including the ancient cities of Bukhara and Samarqand.

Uzbekistan is a world-class producer of cotton. It was colonized by the Russians in the nineteenth century mainly as a cotton plantation. The USSR exploited Uzbekistan's valley and steppe soils and its long growing seasons primarily for the extraction of cotton. Cotton farming has led to Uzbekistan's infamous environmental problems: It has been responsible for the destruction of habitats, poisoning soils, polluting rivers, and killing the Aral Sea. The most common work in Uzbekistan is in the cotton fields. Rural villagers grow and gather the cotton on collective farms officially called "privatized." Workable plots can indeed be granted by a farm manager to a family farmer with increasing needs. However, private land use is restricted and revocable. The market for produce is local, and water is granted, not sold. Their pay is small by any standard. Fortunately, their communities are close knit, so many friends and family are close.

Uzbekistan does have large gold reserves and enough petroleum to power itself for decades to come. Industrial modernization has been slow to catch on here, though, and foreign investors are commonly frustrated by corruption and curious bureaucratic complications. Despite the official government's stated goal of economic reform, cotton production is the mass employer. In fact, 60 percent of the population is rural, compared to only 25 percent in industrialized Europe. Cotton therefore provides a relief valve for the government. It keeps disgruntled poor people from organizing or concentrating in close proximity to the halls of power because raw cotton can be processed only at government-controlled processing centers. The real money comes after that. Where the money goes, no one is quite sure, but the wealth seen in the capital, Tashkent, is far beyond the rural standard of living.

Uzbekistan is the region's major political center, so trends and frictions there foretell regional developments. President Islam Karimov has ruled Uzbekistan with almost total authority since the republics gained independence in 1991. The 12 provinces of Uzbekistan, rather than enabling governance closer to the people, are used to administer edicts handed down from the president. Legislative and judicial leaders of Uzbekistan all support the president. Karimov has been reelected twice by incredible (9 to 1) margins, and his current term has been extended. Opposing political parties have been practically eliminated. Many of the president's political rivals have fled the country or ceased to be politically active. As a result, the primary political opposition is a radicalized Islamist underground, whose main objective is to overthrow the president and install a puritanical regime that probably would not allow dissent either. The next presidential election is scheduled for December 2007. If it is conducted as suspiciously as the past two, observers wonder if the response might not be yet another popular uprising. Uzbekistan bears watching.

Tajikistan

Independence has not come easily to Tajikistan, where the old Soviet policy of building codependent economies is very apparent. For example, Tajikistan is arguably the poorest of all of the former Soviet republics, yet it is also home to mammoth dams whose power output dwarfs the country's needs. To use this power, a huge aluminum industry was placed in Soviet Tajikistan, whose output is of little use to the Tajik people. Tajikistan also has huge uranium reserves, yields from which are entirely exported. Now that Tajikistan is independent and isolated in the core of Asia, its future as an advanced industrial power appears problematic at best.

Soon after the demise of the USSR, Tajikistan sank into civil war, with competing sides fighting either for democracy or for

Islamism. Five years, 50,000 deaths, and half a million refugees later, neither side prevailed. The country's critical infrastructure was badly damaged, and productivity has declined sharply. About 60 percent of Tajikistan's 7 million people live in abject poverty.

Tajikistan has settled into a somewhat regionally fragmented condition with minimal rule from the central government in Dushanbe. The most important crop is still cotton. Twenty-five percent of the population is Uzbek, and there are more Tajiks in Afghanistan than in Tajikistan. Obviously, borders are weak. When the Soviets withdrew from Afghanistan in 1989, Tajikistan's southern border became a frontline barrier against Islamic insurgents. For Russia today, Afghanistan could become a "second Afghanistan"—a conflict they could ill-afford to lose.

Turkmenistan

At the southern extreme of the former Soviet Union, sharing a long border with Iran and Afghanistan, is the desert country of Turkmenistan. The Turkmen were nomadic herders and, in 1884, became the last people to be conquered by the Russian Empire. They are still organized and divided by tribes, and their cities and village networks center on oases. Family is paramount here, where travel is rare and youngsters typically have never used a telephone.

Turkmenistan is amazingly dry and water dependent, and practically all of its water comes from outside the country. Water demands are largely met (and exceeded) by the enormous Karakum Canal. This canal diverts almost half of Central Asia's greatest river, the Amu Dar'ya, from its natural course—emptying into the Aral Sea. With this water, the 5 million Turkmen meet their municipal needs and grow thirsty cotton for export. This water is notoriously wasted, even though the resulting water shortage is killing the Aral Sea and people who live near the end of the Amu Dar'ya.

Turkmenistan has a great wealth of oil and gas, but its land-locked situation is a real barrier to economic development. Currently, Turkmenistan is heavily dependent on Russian pipelines and Ukrainian gas purchases, but deals are in the works for alternative export routes through Iran or Afghanistan and Pakistan. Turkmenistan's natural gas profits no longer disappear in Moscow, and they may serve to finance Turkmenistan's economic reform.

Turkmenistan has one of the world's most colorful and despotic rulers, President Saparmurat Niyazov. When the Soviet Union collapsed, Niyazov, then the Communist Party leader of Turkmenistan, assumed the role of high patriot, *Turkmenbashi*—"father of Turkmen." His picture was printed on the money, and his name was attached to streets, schools, and factories. He also extended his eight-year presidential term to life. He renamed the national airport, Turkmenistan's second-largest city, and the month of January all for himself. He dedicated the year 2003 and every April to his mother. He also banned the ballet, nature reserves, and even the circus. Murals and statues of him abound, including a big gold one in Ashgabat that turns so that it always faces the sun.

President Niyazov's "cult of personality" might seem bizarre to someone from a country where leaders are held more accountable. Surely he gives comfort to other regional dictators. He also clearly constrains the Turkmen people, and print and broadcast media are dominated by news of the president, and it is illegal to oppose him. Street corner cameras watch for "disorder." Dissidents are jailed for "sowing doubt." At least 20,000 of Niyazov's political opponents have been imprisoned, and the torture of many is well documented. The *Ruhnama* (a holy guidebook for the Turkmen) is a collection of Turkmenbashi's thoughts on philosophy, ethics, and culture, and it forms the basis of school curricula. Even to pass a driving test, Turkmen must show knowledge of the *Ruhnama*.

CHAPTER 9

Looking Ahead

Away from downtown Moscow, it can sometimes seem as though little has changed for the average Russian. In the tsarist era (before 1917), less than 10 percent of Russians served in the imperial court. The rest of the population, the poor peasants, just scraped by. In the Soviet era, barely 10 percent of the people joined the Communist Party. They were rewarded with opportunities in politics, entertainment, academia, science, and industry, while the rest of the population just got by. Now, with the fall of the USSR, there has arisen a small concentration of insiders, mainly politicos and the powerful biznismen, whose work is not visible so much for what it does as for what it brings. The rest of the people barter and moonlight, go to the factory when there is work, await their pay, grow and brew what they can, and otherwise just get by. The two populations have little in common.

The concentration of insiders is growing, however, especially among young people. There is, by any account, a new middle class of business people that is making and spending money like Russia has never seen before. The trend is toward upward mobility, and Russia is a very changed place. Most young entrepreneurs cannot remember the Soviet Union, and they know nothing of a time when the government promised so much intervention in peoples' lives. They are training, relocating, and working their way up. They speak their mind, and more and more they speak it in English. A few million young Russians have left the country and are doing well in the West, working in services, education, and technology. None of this was possible before Gorbachev's reforms in the late 1980s. Their parents' world is fundamentally gone. They are charting a new course.

It is true that the government has recently trimmed freedoms of the press and that political opponents increasingly have been censored. It is also true, however, that the Russian president now has a popularity rating that can go both up *and* down. After the 2004 election scandal in Ukraine, it went down. This simply was not a concern before the breakup of the USSR.

Recent polls indicate that Russians are still unsettled about the loss of their great empire. Many imagine a plot by the West to weaken their nation and raid the mineral wealth of the old USSR. They cite the expansion of NATO and the European Union into Russia's former colonies as proof. Economic reforms demanded by the West did not fix anything very quickly. In 2005, a fabulous run-up in energy prices has pulled more than $200 billion into Russia's capital reserves, making it decidedly less sick and more influential on the world stage. Russia's foreign policy is again assuming a skeptical or even antagonistic position toward U.S. concerns in East Asia and toward the Arab world.

Into the twenty-first century, Russia continues to interfere in Moldovan, Ukrainian, and Georgian internal disputes—all to protect its old sphere of influence. Ironically, Russia may be undercutting its own efforts to restore an exclusive trade and security zone. Russia's own heavy-handed actions may chase its old territories toward the European Union, toward a greater Turkish or Islamic movement, and even into closer relations with the United States.

The Russian agenda is full. It is establishing international alliances in a world of fast-changing economic models and shifting ideologies. It is trying to keep the country together while respecting minority rights. It is stimulating the economy and settling on an acceptable degree of government intervention. Personal freedom is being embraced within a tightly managed democracy. The environment needs to be cleaned up. Both the government and citizens are adjusting to the idea of accumulating wealth. This is an exciting yet unsettling time for Russians. They have been here before, and if the last 1,000 years are any indication, Russia will survive and thrive.

860	The Varangians send Rurik to lead the Eastern Slavs, called the Rus.
880	Oleg moves the capital of the Varangian-Rus culture to Kiev; Kievan Rus is born.
988	Vladimir the Great leads his people into the Dnieper River and has them baptized as Orthodox Christians.
1054	The death of Yaroslav the Wise leaves Kievan Rus weakened.
1300	Tatar-Mongol horsemen invade from the east and conquer most of Kievan Rus by this time; the Mongol-Turkic conquerors from north of China go on to dominate lands deep into Europe.
1250–1490	The Russians endure the "Mongol yoke," 240 years of control by Asian Khans.
1480	Russians drive the Turkic-Mongol Empire off of their southern flank by capturing the Oka River, only 70 miles south of Moscow.
1552 and 1556	Led by Tsar Ivan IV, Russians defeat the Mongol Turks at Kazan and Astrakhan, giving the Russians control of the Volga River.
1650	From the Volga River, Russians expand eastward and conquer lands all the way to the Pacific Ocean in less than 100 years.
1703	Tsar Peter the Great drives Germanic tribes westward and establishes the Russian presence on the Baltic Sea coastline; Peter founds a new capital: St. Petersburg; Russia seeks a closer relationship with Western Europe.
1787	Empress Catherine the Great tours the newly captured Crimean Peninsula; Russia now holds lands from the Baltic Sea to the Black Sea.
1812	French Emperor Napoleon invades Russia and loses his great army in the process; Russians retreat to the Volga basin, thus pulling the French so far into Russia that they cannot free themselves from winter's grip.
1861	Alexander II emancipates the serfs; there is little change, however, in the lot of Russia's peasantry.
1865–1881	Russia conquers the Central Asian kingdoms; the tribal kingdoms are combined into a unit called Turkistan, which later become Soviet republics and then the independent states of Kazakhstan, Kyrgyzstan, Uzbekistan, Tajikistan, and Turkmenistan.

1905   Tsar Nicholas II survives a revolution and responds with cautious reforms; he ignores widespread dissatisfaction with his rule.

March and October 1917   Two revolutions overthrow Tsar Nicholas II and seat the Bolsheviks, led by Lenin and Trotsky and their band of Communists.

1920s and 1930s   The USSR carries out a course of rapid and harsh economic reforms, including the collectivization of all means of production; famine ensues and citizens who resist are commonly eliminated; 15 million people die as a result.

August 1939   Soviet leader Joseph Stalin and German leader Adolf Hitler sign a nonaggression pact, enabling the two leaders to take over all lands between them; the USSR seizes Bessarabia (Eastern Romania), the eastern third of Poland, and the Baltic States—Estonia, Latvia, and Lithuania.

June 1941   The nonaggression pact is shattered when Hitler attacks the Soviet Union and occupies much of the western USSR for five years; 20 million Soviet soldiers and civilians die in this war.

1953   Communist Party General Secretary, and the leader of the USSR, Joseph Stalin dies, leaving behind a heritage of military-industrial development, hard police-state rule, and dictatorship over neighboring Central European nations.

1962   The Cuban Missile Crisis brings the Soviet Union and the United States close to nuclear war when the Soviets begin to deploy offensive missiles on Cuba; the Soviet missiles are withdrawn and American missiles likewise are withdrawn from Turkey.

1980–1989   The Soviet Army invades Afghanistan in order to shore up the Soviet-allied government there; a huge guerrilla resistance movement of Mujahideen is assisted by many governments in the Islamic World and the West; the Soviet military eventually withdraws in defeat.

1983   The last leader of the USSR, Mikhail Gorbachev, undertakes radical economic and political reform in an effort to resuscitate the Soviet Union; freedom of speech unleashes a time of expression, then a long period of public complaining, followed by a social depression.

April 26, 1986 The explosion of reactor number 4 at the Chernobyl nuclear power plant in Ukraine spreads toxic levels of radiation over vast territories of northern Ukraine and southern Belarus; the credibility of the Soviet government suffers, as it is seen to be slow acknowledging and responding to the disaster.

December 11, 1988 A devastating earthquake in Armenia kills 25,000 people, leaves half a million homeless, and exposes the Soviet government to widespread charges of corrupt building practices and weak disaster planning.

1991 Gorbachev's reforms fail to fix the Soviet economy, and he barely survives a military overthrow; social divisions force the USSR to dissolve, and 15 constituent republics emerge as independent states; the "Cold War" apparently ends.

1990s Russia moves in a haphazard fashion toward a decentralized market economy; President Boris Yeltsin balances the competing ideologies of newer market democrats and older state-support socialists.

2000–2005 Russian President Vladimir Putin seems to signal a go-slow approach to democracy, a free press, and the rights of business owners to invest or move wealth as they please; Russia continues to balance its foreign policies between improved ties with Western democracies and a system of alliances based on Russia's ability to maintain its sphere of influence with a range of foreign nations and states and customers for its energy, hardware, and expertise.

2003–2005 Former Soviet republics Georgia, Ukraine, and Kyrgyzstan experience popular uprisings; their first-generation post-Soviet authoritarian regimes are replaced with leaderships that generally promise greater democracy and reaffirm their separation from Russia; Uzbekistan has large-scale street protests against the government and responds with deadly force.

BOOKS

Bremmer, Ian, and Taras, Ray, eds. *Nations and Politics in the Soviet Successor States.* London: Cambridge University Press, 1993.

Conquest, Robert. *The Harvest of Sorrow.* New York: Oxford University Press, 1986.

Gilbert, Martin. *Atlas of Russian History.* Great Britain: Dorset Press, 1972.

Government Committee of the USSR for Statistics. *The USSR in Figures, 1988.* Moscow: Finances and Statistics, 1989.

Shabad, Theodore. *Geography of the USSR.* New York: Columbia University Press, 1951.

Shaw, Denis J.B. *Russia in the Modern World: A New Geography.* Oxford, UK: Blackwell Publishers, 1999.

Wixman, Ronald. *The Peoples of the USSR.* Armonk, NY: M.E. Sharpe, 1984.

The World Factbook. Washington, DC: U.S. Central Intelligence Agency.

Zenkovsky, Serge, ed. *Medieval Russia's Epics, Chronicles, and Tales.* New York: E.P. Dutton, 1974.

WEBSITE

Radio Free Europe/Radio Liberty.org

BOOKS

Aslund, Anders, and Martha Brill Olcott, eds. *Russia After Communism.* Washington, DC: Carnegie Endowment for International Peace, 1999.

Feshbach, Murray. *Ecological Disaster: Cleaning Up the Hidden Legacy of the Soviet Regime.* New York: Twentieth Century Fund Press, 1995.

Gorbachev, Mikhail Sergeevich. *On My Country and the World.* New York: Columbia University Press, 2000.

Remnick, David. *Lenin's Tomb.* New York: Vintage Books, 1993.

Smith, Hedrick. *The New Russians.* New York: Random House, 1990.

Solzhenitsyn, Alexander. *One Day in the Life of Ivan Denisovich.* New York: E.P. Dutton & Co., 1963.

JOURNAL

Eurasian Geography and Economics. Columbia, MD: Bellwether Publishing.

WEBSITES

Johnson's Russia List
www.cdi.org/russia/johnson/default/cfm

Pravda.Ru
http://english.pravda.ru/

U.S. Commerce Department BISNIS Bulletin
http://www.bisnis.doc.gov/bisnis/bulletin.cfm

U.S. State Department Background Note: Russia
www.state.gov/r/pa/ei/bgn/3183.htm

page:

THOMAS MCCRAY, Ph.D., is an instructor at Columbia College in Columbia, Missouri, and at the University of Missouri. His main interests are cultural and economic and physical geography. He lectures on Southwest Asia and nations and regions of the former Soviet Union. His research has involved circumnavigations of South America, sailing on Siberia's Lake Baikal, farming and railroading in California's San Joaquin Valley, and studying post-Soviet reforms among the Central Asian states.

CHARLES F. "FRITZ" GRITZNER is Distinguished Professor of Geography at South Dakota University in Brookings. He is now in his fifth decade of college teaching and research. During his career, he has taught more than 60 different courses, spanning the fields of physical, cultural, and regional geography. In addition to his teaching, he enjoys writing, working with teachers, and sharing his love for geography with students. As consulting editor for the MODERN WORLD CULTURES series, he has a wonderful opportunity to combine each of these "hobbies." Fritz has served as both President and Executive Director of the National Council for Geographic Education and has received the Council's highest honor, the George J. Miller Award for Distinguished Service. In March 2004, he won the Distinguished Teaching award from the Association of American Geographers at their annual meeting in Philadelphia.